RICHARD C. YOUNG'S
FINANCIAL ARMADILLO STRATEGY

RICHARD C. YOUNG'S
FINANCIAL ARMADILLO STRATEGY

RICHARD C. YOUNG
with DAVID FRANKE

WILLIAM MORROW AND COMPANY, INC.
• NEW YORK •

Library of Congress Cataloging-in-Publication Data

Young, Richard C. (Richard Carlyle), 1940–
Richard C. Young's financial armadillo strategy.

Includes index.
1. Investments. I. Franke, David.   II. Title.
III. Title: Financial armadillo strategy.
HG4521.Y58   1987   332.6'78   86-16446
ISBN 0-688-05830-2

Printed in the United States of America

2 3 4 5 6 7 8 9 10

BOOK DESIGN BY ELLEN LOGIUDICE

To my wife, Debbie,
and
my children, Matt and Becky

Contents

Tables

Preface

The only thing that's certain in the financial world is that everything will change. Stock quotations change constantly on the Big Board, the mood of the market shifts as fast as the wind, and even general economic conditions seem to turn without warning.

When change is the only certainty, how can the individual investor plan rationally for his or her personal financial growth? How can you pursue profits—with all the risk that pursuit entails in a constantly changing environment—and still protect your capital?

I have grappled with this problem ever since I entered the investment business in 1964. I constantly sought ways to insulate portfolios from the various shocks that continually hit the marketplace. A large part of the problem, familiar to every investor, was that the safest investments brought minimal returns—and often negative returns, when you took inflation into account. You had to choose between safety or growth. You couldn't have both.

Until now.

Suddenly, in the 1980s, a dramatic shift has altered the economic structure of the United States. I am referring to the massive deficits of the federal government.

Everyone else has been so busy debating the political aspects of these deficits that they have missed their significance for the investor. I grasped that significance because I knew what I was looking for all these years. I have built an investment strategy around this revolutionary and historic change, and I call it the "Financial Armadillo Strategy." This strategy has been making money for my clients, who range from ordinary individuals in all walks of life to top business executives, some of the most prestigious and successful *Fortune* 500 corporations, and international banks. Now, for the first time, I am offering this opportunity to you as well.

My Financial Armadillo Strategy shows you how to pursue and capture big profits—with all the risk that entails—and still sleep soundly at night. You can do this because my Financial Armadillo Strategy also erects a safety net around your principal that gives you more financial protection than was ever before possible.

No previous investment strategy—no other book in your financial library—has offered you such extraordinary safety of principal while you pursue megaprofits in what I call "The Big Game Hunt." They couldn't, because it just has not been possible until now.

This protection only became possible with the changes Uncle Sam's deficits imposed on the financial markets. And the deficits are not going to disappear for some time. On the contrary, they are now growing even in times of economic recovery, and even the most optimistic forecast (from the administration in power, of course) admits they are going to be larger at the end of this decade than anything ever seen before the 1980s. Ironically, though, it is thanks to these horrendous deficits that you can stop worrying (as an investor, at least) about whether the future will bring us boom or bust, inflation or deflation.

While innovative in its concept, my Financial Armadillo Strategy is remarkable in its simplicity. It uses very familiar types of investments—notably U.S. Treasury securities, gold, mutual funds, and individual stocks. Nothing esoteric there. Obviously, people have been investing in them for years. The revolutionary difference is *how* you use them—how you combine them into a personal strategy that serves your needs and goals, and how the strategy changes with corresponding changes in the economic cycle. Even here, there is nothing difficult to understand. I won't hand you complicated mathematical formulas or econometric models. All it will take on your part is the thoughtful attention you *should* give to your financial future.

But why, you may wonder, did I pick the armadillo as the namesake for my strategy? After all, many people think of it as a rather funny creature. I'll grant you that the armadillo is no flashy peacock, but it does have some amazing qualities that I think should be important to you as an investor. I like to say that these qualities make the armadillo an all-weather fighter, good on both the defense and the offense. The armadillo is like those old-time football greats who played on both sides of the line of scrimmage.

The Defensive Parallel: The Armadillo's Protective Coat of Armor

From head to tail, top to bottom, the armadillo is covered by a coat of armor that protects it from its natural adversaries. All it has to do is curl up into a ball when it's in danger.

My Financial Armadillo Strategy provides as much protection for the investor as that coat of armor provides for the armadillo. It does this by giving you:
1. *real* profits that outpace inflation
2. absolute safety of principal
3. a safety net against potential price inflation
4. similar protection against potential price deflation.

The Aggressive Parallel: The Armadillo's Sharp Claws

Despite its coat of armor, the armadillo is not merely passive. It has extremely sharp claws, too.

My Financial Armadillo Strategy is as aggressive in its search for profits as the armadillo is in its search for food.

Let me give just one example now, to whet your appetite. Among the investments I track carefully and regularly are the Merrill Lynch stock options. As with all of the Financial Armadillo's aggressive investments, you have to know *when* in the economic cycle to buy, and when to sell. If you had followed my timing advice the last time around—advice I'll give you in Chapter 9—you could have watched an $8,750 investment grow to $405,125 in only thirteen weeks. *These are exact figures,* taken from a Financial Armadillo's case history, and give you a real-life example of what can happen when there's a major turn in the business cycle.

For an added bonus, as a Financial Armadillo, you wouldn't

have shed your coat of armor—your protected capital—in order to take the risk that is *always* inherent in options.

The Armadillo as a Survivor

Thanks to this unique combination of a built-in coat of armor and an extremely sharp set of claws, the armadillo is a survivor. It is one of the oldest animals on earth. While thousands of other species have become extinct, the armadillo traces its family tree back to prehistoric times, when its ancestor, the glyptodont, was as big as an ox and armed with a spiked club at the end of its tail that could tear apart a saber-toothed tiger!

In the financial jungle, too, investment fads and fashions get the headlines for a day, and then crash—like so many extinct dodos. *Like its namesake, the Financial Armadillo ignores these fads and uses its coat of armor and claws not only to survive, but to prosper year after year, through fad after investment fad.*

I have already alluded to the importance of timing. That's true for the mammalian armadillo too. It uses timing to its best advantage. For one thing, it's a nocturnal creature with good eyes, so it ventures out at night when its adversaries are asleep or can't see that well.

Like the armadillo, you have to know when to go on the offensive and when to stick to the defensive. Details, as I say, will come in Chapter 9. There I will show you how to tell where you stand in the economic cycle—whether the economy is gaining momentum, losing momentum, or fast approaching a recession. Those are the critical turning points that call for changes in the mix of your Financial Armadillo Strategy.

As important as these changes in the economic cycle are the changes in your life. That's why, in Chapter 14, I will show you how to apply the Financial Armadillo Strategy at different stages of your life—when you graduate from school and enter the business world, during your financial growth years, during your peak earning and pre-retirement years, and when actually in retirement. Circumstances change throughout your lifetime, and by taking these changes into account, my Financial Armadillo Strategy becomes your *lifetime* road map for financial success.

If You Can't Predict the Future,
Why Try to Do It—and Bet Money on It?

The question of timing brings us directly to the matter of what the future is going to bring.

Most investment strategies fail because they try to predict the future. When those predictions go wrong (as they inevitably do), the profits you were counting on rarely materialize. Often they disappear entirely. If you're lucky, you get to keep your shirt.

The inescapable truth is that none of us can predict the future. *Not a single one of us has tomorrow's newspapers.* Not you, not me, and not anyone else.

To remind myself of this, I always keep a couple of examples pinned to my bulletin board. One of these is an article from the June 6, 1984 *Wall Street Journal.* In this article, a man who has devised one of the most prestigious econometric models revised his forecast for second quarter real gross national product (GNP) "all the way down to zero." This was, mind you, just twenty-four days before the completion of the year's second quarter.

So what happened? GNP growth in the second quarter of 1984 was up 7.5 percent. Score 100 percent wrong for one of the major econometric models! And let's hope you weren't basing your plans on this man's zero-growth forecast.

My other current bulletin board pinup is actually someone I admire quite a bit—Nobel laureate Milton Friedman. I have learned a great deal from him, yet here he is in the December 12, 1983, issue of *Business Week,* predicting a recession in 1984 if the money supply doesn't pick up its pace. Well, you know what happened—the money supply collapsed, and we still had a terrific recovery. If Milton Friedman can't predict the future, who can?

At this point, it would be fair for you to turn the tables on me and demand to know how I, Dick Young, presume to tell my clients what the future is going to bring. After all, my principal publication is called *Young's World Money Forecast.* Am I going to be a nitpicker and try to distinguish between a "forecast" and a "prediction"? No, I won't. On the contrary, I have to admit that the word "forecast" is a misnomer in describing my work. The critical difference between me and the prognosticators, as I see it, is that I seek to tell my clients and readers what is happening right now—where we stand in the economic cycle today. And believe me, it's hard enough trying to figure out what's happening today, much less tomorrow!

Of course, this is no mere academic exercise on my part. I'm advising my clients on how to make money. To do that, I make detailed comparisons with previous economic cycles. Each cycle has its own fingerprint, but much of what has gone on in the past has a bearing on what goes on in the future. Cycles don't repeat in the exact same way, but they do repeat in similar ways.

Even so, I make specific projections for only the next quarter or two. Nobody can stretch this sort of analysis out for a year or two and still maintain enough accuracy to make it worthwhile. I've been in the financial advisory business all of my adult life, and I have never found a single individual equal to that superhuman task. Even vast government bureaucracies, with all the resources at their disposal, are not equal to the task! The battlefield is strewn with the reputations of people forecasting one and two and three years ahead.

For the intelligent investor, moreover, there is no *need* to know the future in order to prosper. If you have an accurate picture of what is happening now, and what is likely to happen in the next three to six months, you are far ahead of the game. This is particularly true for the Financial Armadillo. The defensive part of your strategy is set up to prosper whichever way the economy turns. And the aggressive part of your strategy requires only that you know what is happening today.

With that in mind, let's look first at each of the major elements of the Financial Armadillo Strategy, and then put them together to make you some money.

· INTRODUCTION ·

The Basic Elements of the Financial Armadillo Strategy

It was way back in 1973 that I first thought of the armadillo as the symbol of what I was seeking. I knew what I was looking for—a portfolio that would be the financial equivalent of the armadillo's coat of armor and claws, a linked strategy that would protect your capital while you aggressively sought out profits. But I couldn't find that rugged match in the financial world, no matter how I searched. Strategies with a strong offense were weak in the defense, or just the reverse. The combination that would win me the financial Super Bowl wasn't around.

Then, in the 1980s, the federal government's massive deficits changed all that. The budget went out of control, and raising taxes to cover the deficits was out of the question. In those circumstances, the government had to raise those gargantuan sums through the sale of government bonds—U.S. Treasury securities.

The process was nothing new. Treasury securities have been around for as long as there's been red ink. The big difference was the *amount* of money that had to be raised in this way. All of a sudden, Uncle Sam had to offer a better deal if he wanted to attract new buyers.

There was another difference. By 1980, people had become inflation-wise. Everyone realized that to come out ahead, you had to make more money than you lost through inflation. The *nominal* or face-value return on any investment was no longer the key. What you looked for was the *real* rate of return—how much of a return your investment brings after subtracting the amount lost to inflation.

Over the twenty-year period from 1953 to 1973, the normal range of inflation-adjusted return for five-year Treasury notes was between 0.5 and 3.5 percent. A 2 percent inflation premium was a pretty good benchmark. With a return like that, you can see why most buyers of Treasury securities were institutions seeking bedrock safety rather than hefty profits.

The situation became even worse in the 1970s. The real return on Treasury securities went *negative* in 1974, and stayed that way until 1980. Hardly a way to protect and increase your capital!

Enter the 1980s. Faced with unprecedented deficits and a need to raise more than one hundred billion dollars a year, Uncle Sam had to sweeten the pot—a lot. And when he did, he found a huge new pool of buyers—individuals buying Treasury securities in thousand-dollar denominations, rather than just institutions that counted by the millions. And these individual buyers came from all corners of the globe.

As I write, the yield on five-year Treasury notes is 7.46 percent, and inflation is 1.5 percent. Your inflation-adjusted return (your *real* rate of return) on five-year Treasury notes is thus an impressive 6.0 percent. *There is no example before the 1980s of such a high real rate of return—not for a security carrying the gilt-edged safety of a Treasury note!*

But Uncle Sam had done more than attract the buyers he needed. He also provided me with the missing link for my Financial Armadillo Strategy.

Part I of the Financial Armadillo Strategy: A Protective Coat of Armor for Your Principal

The World's Safest Investment

I call U.S. Treasury bills and short-term notes the world's safest investment. That's a pretty big plus, but it isn't everything. As long as they brought a negative real rate of return, they could hardly be considered for a strategy to protect *and increase* your capital, no matter how safe.

As we've seen, though, it's a different ballgame now. Since Treasury securities now make sense financially, we can take a second look at their most formidable quality—their safety.

Why do I call them the world's safest investment? Because

they come as close as possible to giving you absolute security of principal. Treasury securities are backed by the full taxing power of the federal government. Thus, the interest payments and the return of principal are fully guaranteed. The U.S. government is legally obligated to you, the purchaser.

When you buy Treasury securities, you are lending Uncle Sam money to cover the federal government's mammoth budget deficit and to pay off maturing issues of Treasury bills, notes, and bonds. For the use of your money, Uncle Sam pays you interest. The amount of interest varies according to each issue, and is determined by the bidding for that issue.

I am fully aware that theoretically the U.S. government *could* default on its obligations. But the penalty to the United States and to the world would be too huge for that to be considered. One default, and all investors would abandon Treasury securities overnight. The major source of meeting the government's deficit would dry up. The U.S. government would be admitting to bankruptcy, and the repercussion would be nothing less than worldwide financial collapse. Given such a choice— between continuing to pay interest to purchasers of Treasury securities, and economic collapse—you can see why it really isn't a choice at all.

At the height of our recent bout with double-digit inflation, many overzealous "gold bugs"—and a lot of others, too—talked as if the world was indeed coming apart, with the U.S. government leading the parade. Now that times have calmed down, we can see just how silly that notion is. I'm not saying we don't have problems. We have *major* economic and political problems facing us as a nation, and the federal deficit is just one of them. But the dissolution of the government is *not* one of them, and short of Armageddon the government's Treasury securities remain the safest place you can park your money.

If you don't believe me, ask a foreigner. In some recent years, foreign funds may have accounted for as much as half of all net investment in the United States. In late 1985, *U.S. News & World Report* stated that "foreign corporations have spent almost 16 billion dollars to buy U.S. companies this year. . . . That's just a fraction of foreign holdings in this country. Purchases of U.S. government securities, joint ventures with U.S. companies and real-estate investments are all on the rise. The foreign stake in the U.S. could reach 1 trillion dollars by 1986."

For better or for worse, the United States is the world's foremost bastion of capitalism.

In a later chapter, I will discuss in greater detail why Financial Armadillos love Treasury securities, what kinds are available (and which ones you should choose), how to buy them, and how to use them as part of your lifetime road map for financial independence.

The World's Premier Inflation Hedge— and Store of Value

Financial Armadillos also love gold. There is good cause for this love affair: *Throughout history, gold has been the world's premier hedge against inflation.*

In Chapter 3, we will look at gold's unique performance over the centuries and compare gold's recent inflation-hedging performance with the performance of other assets. For now, I'd like to show you how the price of gold has outpaced the rate of inflation itself in recent years. I think you'll be impressed.

Gold has had two major bull markets during the past two decades—in 1971–74 and again in 1976–80. In addition to the bull markets for gold, these periods had three economic characteristics in common:

1. A substantial hike in oil prices

2. A significant increase in the *underlying* rate of inflation (gains in average hourly earnings, adjusted for productivity)

3. Jumps in *price* inflation, as measured by the U.S. Consumer Price Index (CPI).

Table 1 shows how gold performed in response to inflation during those years.

No further proof is needed! In both periods, the rise in the price of gold protected you from inflation—both the underlying rate of inflation and consumer price inflation. Indeed, gold did more than protect you—it provided hefty profits.

While price inflation increased 253 percent from 1971 to 1974, jumping into double-digit rates, gold's price increased a whopping 427 percent during the same period. And while price inflation jumped 233 percent from 1976 to 1980, again rising to double-digit rates, gold did even slightly better than before—its price rose 437 percent.

TABLE 1
Gold and Inflation,
1971–74 and 1976–80

	OIL ($/BARREL)	UNDERLYING RATE OF INFLATION	U.S. CPI	GOLD ($/OUNCE)
1971	$1.65	3.4%	4.3%	$ 43.63
1972	1.90	2.3	3.3	64.90
1973	2.70	7.1	6.3	112.25
1974	9.76	10.2	10.9	186.50
1971–74 % Change	+592%	+300%	+253%	+427%
1976	$11.51	5.3%	5.8%	$134.75
1977	12.40	5.6	6.5	164.95
1978	12.70	8.5	7.5	226.00
1979	16.97	9.5	11.3	512.00
1980	28.67	8.8	13.5	589.50
1976–80 % Change	+249%	+166%	+233%	+437%

Don't be misled by gold's lackluster performance in recent years. The years since 1980 have witnessed a dramatic, if temporary, turnaround on inflation, and the price of gold reflects the direction of inflation over the long term. Actually, gold's price has decreased *less* than the rate of inflation—it has retained its value better than you might expect. To see this, let's update our information and look at Table 2 on page 22.

Even after these charts, you may be surprised to see gold playing such a prominent role in the protective part of our strategy. After the flurry of bankruptcies and frauds that hit the industry in the '80s, many find it hard to think of gold as anything but a risky speculation. But there are right ways and wrong ways to buy any asset, and in Chapter 3 I'll tell you the right ways to buy gold. *How* you buy can sometimes be as important as *what* you buy.

In summary: Gold is not a way to get rich in all seasons, but it *is* without match as insurance against the ravages of inflation.

TABLE 2
Gold and Inflation,
1980–85

	OIL ($/BARREL)	UNDERLYING RATE OF INFLATION	U.S. CPI	GOLD ($/OUNCE)
1980	$28.67	8.8%	13.5%	$589.50
1981	32.50	7.5	10.4	397.50
1982	33.45	1.6	6.2	456.90
1983	28.60	0.0	3.8	382.40
1984	28.47	0.4	4.0	308.30
1985	28.00	2.7	3.8	327.00
1980–85 % Change	−2.4%	−69.3%	−71.9%	−44.5%

And that is why it is part of our Financial Armadillo Strategy.

For reasons I'll present in Chapter 4, I think silver also deserves consideration for the precious metals portion of your portfolio. There is no need to develop those reasons here, just to note that silver *complements* your gold insurance but never substitutes for it.

Treasury Securities and Gold Together: The Financial Armadillo's Coat of Armor

Treasury securities and gold—combined in the right proportions, like the plates that shield the armadillo's body—constitute a financial coat of armor that protects your principal more effectively than any other strategy ever devised. Let's take a quick look at the reason they work so well together.

Gold is essential to the Financial Armadillo Strategy because of the protection it provides your assets against inflation. As we've seen, you can expect the gold portion of your portfolio to jump dramatically in value with any significant increase in the rate of inflation. If, on the other hand, inflation goes down, it's your Treasury securities that increase in value. The purchasing power of their fixed yield is enhanced as goods and services are offered in the marketplace at reduced prices.

By mixing these two *in the right proportion,* therefore, you have equally ironclad protection against rising inflation, decreasing inflation, or even downright deflation. *No other strategy offers such all-weather protection—and growth—for your principal!*

In Chapter 5, I'll show you how to figure out, simply and precisely, what that mix should be at any stage of the economic cycle and during all stages of your lifetime. For now, let's look at what the Financial Armadillo Strategy has to offer you in the way of an aggressive search for profits.

Part II of the Financial Armadillo Strategy: Sharp Claws Aggressively Seeking Profits

In financial circles, the word "investment" has a good connotation, implying sound use of your money and no undue risk. The word "speculation," on the other hand, implies a much greater degree of risk—risk you take for the sake of potentially much greater profits.

I know of no way to distinguish objectively between an investment and a speculation. We are always dealing in *degrees* of risk, and frequently we cannot judge that degree of risk with accuracy. But no matter how anxious you are for a big and quick return, and no matter how big a pile of discretionary funds you have to gamble with, you don't want to throw your money away willy-nilly. You want to use common sense even when speculating.

I can say without equivocation that the protective part of the Financial Armadillo Strategy—the coat of armor consisting of Treasury securities and gold—is the safest place to park your money. No hedging there. From here on out, though, it's much more tricky.

I make a general assessment of the risk involved in different types of investments in "The Financial Armadillo's Investment Rating Chart" (pages 232–233). And in Chapter 14, I provide guidelines for different stages of your lifetime, suggesting what proportion of your funds should be the coat of armor and what proportion should represent your aggressive claws. In the end, though, *you* have to determine your appetite for the Big Bucks—and the risk you are willing to take to get them.

As for myself, I limit the term "investments" to cover my

primary residence or modestly mortgaged summer home, home furnishings, personally owned automobiles, U.S. Treasury bills and notes *(not* long-term bonds), high-grade no-load common stock funds with solid long-term records, modest holdings of gold and silver bullion and related gold coins, high-grade money market funds, and, finally, insured bank deposits. When I venture outside those boundaries, I follow a very simple rule that allows me to sleep soundly at night: I never speculate beyond my ability to lose 100 percent of my speculating capital with a grin.

Lose all of your speculating funds with a grin? Such losses, you say, would have to be small indeed! Yes, but the word "small" is relative. If you earn a million dollars per year and want to gamble with $50,000 of your annual income, most people would agree you're justified in trying your luck. On the other hand, if you earn $25,000 a year, I would consider speculation with even $1,000 to be imprudent. Sure, you might double your $1,000. The likelihood, however, is that you would lose your $1,000 and miss it much more than the millionaire would miss $50,000. Most people are simply not good speculators, and sooner or later they separate themselves from badly needed capital.

Fortunately, you don't have to speculate wildly in order to do very well indeed financially. The timing I discuss in Chapters 9 and 10 is a major key to sharpening your claws and increasing your profits—dramatically. Another way to sharpen your claws is to choose the right vehicle for the type of asset you're buying.

Since most of the "financial claws" I recommend in Chapters 6, 7, and 8 involve stocks, let's apply what I've said to the stock market.

First, the matter of the proper vehicle.

I rarely buy individual stocks. If you are retired or independent, or aren't busy raising a family and running a business (as I am), you may want to be your own stock market analyst. It is a tremendously rewarding exercise if you can devote the proper amount of time to in-depth studies. But for me, no-load mutual funds offer a solid alternative to individual stocks. Another benefit of mutual funds, of course, is the protection they offer in the way of diversification. A handful of individual stocks has to be considered a speculation, no matter which stocks you hold.

There are a large number of mutual funds run by excellent

people who have demonstrated a long-term ability to do well—often spectacularly well. I have made it my business to get to know these people, and to put together portfolios of mutual funds to fit different stock market climates. The best of these funds are the ones I recommend in Chapter 6. In that chapter, I will not only name names, I will also describe the characteristics that make these funds desirable. In that way, you can learn how to switch to other mutual funds as conditions change in the future.

Next, the matter of timing.

For significant profits, timing is all-important. Yes, you can usually come out ahead by placing your money in the right funds and letting it sit there for a long time. But the most dramatic stock market advances come out of the teeth of recession, so for the most impressive financial gains, you have to bite the bullet and commit yourself to the stock market when everyone else is retreating from the bloody battlefield. That's why I aggressively commit funds to the stock market once the economy has declined for two quarters in succession. And that's why I start selling, in a planned fashion, once the bloom is off the boom and the economy starts losing momentum. There are better places to make money then.

Combining the right vehicle with the right timing, I will then show you how and when to switch between different *types* of funds. This ensures that you use each stage of the business cycle to your best advantage. Used in this way, these funds earn their designation as "claws" by their ability to outpace the market dramatically, particularly in a new bull market. For example, the Standard and Poor's (S&P) 500 Common Stock Index rose 44.91 percent in the nine months from June 30, 1982, to March 31, 1983. *During that same period, one of my favorite funds jumped 80.86 percent—almost twice as high as the market in general.*

Of course, this volatility often extends to the downside swings of the market too, so you'll want to pay close attention to my timing advice for selling as well as buying into these funds. I give you the specific track record and timing recommendations for each fund covered in Chapter 6.

Some of the other "financial claws" are pegged more specifically to a resurgence of inflation than to a particular phase of the business cycle. That's why Chapter 10 shows you how to tell what the outlook is for inflation. When the inflationary traffic light turns green, you want to rush into the funds that are set to skyrocket in times of roaring inflation. I tell you what these are in Chapter 6.

These funds do not exhaust our "financial claws." "The big game hunt" is my name for the safari in which you stalk the individual stocks that will soar—and what investor doesn't dream of bagging "the IBM of the future"? Finally, at the right time in the market cycle, aggressive gamblers and traders can have a field day with one of our sharpest but most treacherous financial claws—stock options. These are not for the timid, because when you're wrong with options you lose *all* that you've put in. I can tell you that I personally have taken a 100-percent loss trading options. Most traders do from time to time; it's part of what options are all about—you lose big and you win big. To see why you might want to consider options at all, remember the example I gave you in the Preface—the Financial Armadillo who turned an $8,750 speculation in Merrill Lynch stock options into $405,125 in only thirteen weeks. How's *that* for claws with real profit-grasping power!

With your basic principal protected by a financial coat of armor, you can afford to be as aggressive as you like with your discretionary funds. You can play it relatively safe with mutual funds, catch a little excitement with "the big game hunt," or risk it all on stock options. Whatever your choices, my Financial Armadillo Strategy makes it possible for you to gamble with a clear conscience, and to turn the odds more in your favor.

Part III of the Financial Armadillo Strategy: The Right Mix to Ensure Your Financial Success

The third basic element of my Financial Armadillo Strategy is the proper combination of everything we've already discussed. This is essential if you are to reap maximum profits from the strategy throughout your lifetime. I have already referred several times to this aspect of the strategy, but let's quickly review the different ways in which the right mix is important.

First, in order to get the maximum benefit from your financial coat of armor, it is necessary that you match Treasury securities and gold in the right proportion. I will show you how to do this in Chapter 5.

Second, the extent to which you commit your discretionary funds to your profit-seeking financial claws will depend largely on the current stage of the business cycle. In Chapter 9, I'll show you how to tell where we stand in the business cycle, and how to use this knowledge to multiply your profits. Similarly, in Chapter 10, I will show you how to tell where we stand in the inflationary cycle, and how to use *that* knowledge to multiply your profits. In addition, each of the chapters on our financial claws—Chapters 6, 7, and 8—includes advice on *when* to buy and sell these assets.

Third, you must strike the proper balance between the funds you commit to your financial coat of armor (your protected capital) and the discretionary funds you commit to your more aggressive financial claws. In Chapter 14, I will show you how to do this in each major stage of your adult life—from the time you enter the work force through your retirement years.

You must set your own goals—goals that will vary depending on your age, income, personality, and the funds you have available to invest. But by applying the principles presented in the rest of this book, you can reap maximum profits from the Financial Armadillo Strategy and use it as your lifetime road map to financial success.

· Part I ·
THE FINANCIAL ARMADILLO'S COAT OF ARMOR

· ONE ·

What, Me Worry?

Those of you who are old enough may remember the comic book character from the late 1950s who was known for his imbecilic grin and the caption, "What, Me Worry?" I forget his name, but his name wasn't important. What was important was that dopey grin and the attitude that went with it. He never knew *stress*—that buzzword of the '70s—because he was too *dumb* to worry about anything.

Today, a lot of people who are supposedly quite sophisticated are going around with attitudes that remind me, uncomfortably, of old "What, Me Worry?" It's as unfashionable to be worried about *anything* in the mid-1980s as it was unfashionable in 1980 to think the world might survive.

There are two major reasons, as I see it, for this dramatic turnabout in public attitude.

The first, of course, is President Ronald Reagan. He's so likeable a person that it is difficult for even hardcore Democrats to get riled up over his most outrageous (to them) actions. His cheerily optimistic, can-do attitude was just the tonic the nation needed after the prissy Reverend Carter and the humiliating hostage misfortunes in Iran.

The second reason is inflation. Double-digit inflation was a new and justifiably scary experience for the United States. And as the public sees it, Sir Lancelot Reagan has slain that dragon. The prolonged stock market boom that followed the initial Reagan recession is all the proof many people need that the nation's economic house has been put in order.

I wish it were so. Public fads and fashions rarely reflect reality, however, usually because reality is too complex to fit onto a bumper sticker or a five-minute segment of the evening news. Yes, the nation had enormous problems facing it as we entered the 1980s, but the doomsayers ignored the residual strengths in the economy and the people—strengths that a strong, fresh leader could tap. And yes, the nation does appear, on the surface, to be much better off now, in the mid-'80s. But it bothers me when the surface is covered by a rug—and a pretty lumpy rug at that. Politicians are unsurpassed when it comes to weaving big and handsome rugs, the better to sweep problems under.

Public fads and fashions certainly affect the day-to-day financial markets, and you have to take them into consideration. But the investor who seeks *long-term safety and appreciation* must look beyond today's fads and fashions. Today, the greatest danger is thinking that all our serious economic problems have vanished. As a prudent investor, you'd better look under that lumpy rug.

Inflation: The Lively Corpse

Inflation today is less than it was during the peak double-digit year of 1980, but it still remains at double-digit levels. This is happening, moreover, without the spiraling oil prices that fueled the previous round of inflation. Indeed, as we all know, oil prices have dropped dramatically. These circumstances probably make our current inflation more dangerous than any inflation experienced since the end of World War II.

At this point you're probably ready to throw this book into the trash bin, or demand a refund. Dick Young has apparently been asleep for the past six years! Hasn't he heard that we have brought the inflation rate down to less than two percent?

No, I haven't been asleep during the past six years. Nor have you. But you have been reading the headlines and stories in the popular and business press, while I've been reading the statistics published by the International Monetary Fund. More to the point, the headlines and stories you have read refer to inflation in the United States, while my opening paragraph above refers to *worldwide* inflation.

This parochialism of the popular and business press is curious, to say the least. For all the talk about "the world economy," we act as if much of the world doesn't exist. Unless there's been a great geographical reshuffling in the past few years, the world is still comprised of many countries in addition to the United States, West Germany, Japan, and Switzerland.

When we broaden our horizons, we find that the world is

being flooded with worthless paper at an ever-increasing rate. Moreover, a deepening chasm separates a few industrialized countries from the rest of the world. Most major nations *are* coping with inflation, but many more nations obviously *cannot* cope with it. The implications of this unprecedented divergence are truly frightening.

Back in the 1950s and '60s it was normal for the world inflation rate to hold at about 1 percent above the inflation rate of the industrialized nations. In the '50s, the world inflation rate held below 5 percent. In the '60s, worldwide price inflation never reached 6 percent.

In the 1970s, both the rate of inflation and the gap between the world rate and the industrial nations' rate picked up steam. The world rate moved well into the double digits and hit 15.4 percent in 1974, on the heels of the first oil shock. Inflation in the industrialized countries also picked up momentum, hitting 13.3 percent in 1974. The gap between the world rate and the industrialized countries' rate widened to as much as 3 percent.

After a second round of spiraling oil prices, a new inflationary peak was reached in 1980. That year the worldwide inflation rate was 15.8 percent. The rate in the industrial countries was 11.9 percent, for a gap of almost 4 percent.

Since then the rate of price inflation in the industrial countries has dropped to 2.1 percent. Worldwide, however, the inflation rate never dropped below 12.3 percent. That was in 1982, and as I write it has risen back to 12.8 percent. That's modestly below the 1980 peak of 15.8 percent, and the gap between the industrial countries' rate and the worldwide rate has become a chasm—more than 10 percent.

While I have been referring to price inflation, it should be noted that *over the long run* price inflation follows the direction and pattern of money growth (monetary inflation). In 1970, world money growth was 7.5 percent, only 1.5 percent above the money growth rate in the industrial nations. Today world money growth is 21.0 percent worldwide and 9.9 percent in the industrial nations—a whopping imbalance of 11.1 percent.

For the most part, the worldwide problem is not centered in the oil exporting countries, nor in Africa or Asia. The worst inflationary problems are found in Central and South America. Problems of a lesser but still important degree are found in Europe and the Middle East, with countries such as Israel, Greece,

Portugal, and Yugoslavia suffering from deep-seated inflationary problems.

In the thirty-one Central and South American countries, inflation has jumped from 13 percent in 1970 to 58 percent in 1980 and to more than 110 percent in 1986. This process of doubling and redoubling of the inflation rate is a time bomb, especially when you consider the enormous and ever-growing level of debt in Central and South America. As inflation has taken hold, the currencies of these countries have become increasingly valueless. In Brazil, for example, the 1980 exchange rate was .066 Brazilian cruzados to the dollar. By mid-1986, the official market rate listed by the International Monetary Fund was over 13 cruzados to the dollar, and the black market provided a far more favorable rate of exchange. In just four years the cruzado had lost virtually all of its purchasing power against the U.S. dollar. When you consider that most of Brazil's external debt and raw materials imports are denominated in U.S. dollar terms, *there is no way Brazil can service the interest on its bank debts, much less pay them off.*

Or consider the United States' southern neighbor, Mexico. In the 1950s, '60s, and early '70s, inflation was not an issue in Mexico. As recently as 1972, the Mexican consumer price index was ahead by only 5 percent. Since 1972, however, inflation has been at double-digit levels every year. In 1986, inflation soared at an annual rate above 60 percent. From 1955 through 1975, the Mexican currency held firm at 12.5 pesos to the dollar. In 1976 the roof fell in and the peso collapsed to 20 to the dollar. Today the market rate exceeds 600 pesos to the dollar. In effect, a 1975 peso is virtually worthless today in U.S. dollar terms— or, for that matter, in terms of any of the world's desirable currencies. This means that the billions of pesos accumulated by Mexican businesses and individuals during the 1950s, '60s, and '70s are no longer worth anything in terms of purchasing the desirable products provided by major foreign countries.

The situation is not hopeless, of course—just desperate. Bolivia, formerly the worst economy on the continent, has shown what *can* be done with courage and determination. Its annual rate of inflation had been "only" 32 percent as recently as 1981, but zoomed out of control at 20,000 percent by 1985. Then new president Victor Paz Estenssoro took office and convinced the nation to bite the bullet, bringing inflation back down to 20 percent in one year. Look at what he had to do, though. He had to freeze wages, lift price controls, arrest rebellious union leaders, raise taxes, tackle the pervasive cocaine industry with our help, and above all stop the printing presses. The result is depression for the continent's already-poorest people.

As I write, Mr. Paz Estenssoro is still in office—but who knows about tomorrow? And how many other nations will demonstrate the courage and the will found in Bolivia? The continent's inflationary trends cannot continue unchecked, however, without producing the same kind of intolerable political and economic climate that brought Bolivia to the brink—a brink where depression is the better alternative. Inevitably, the turmoil that Central and South America is bound to experience will affect the United States as well.

Why U.S. Inflation Will Rise Too

There is no doubt that the United States is far better off with an inflation rate of under 2 percent than it was when price inflation hit 14.2 percent during the first quarter of 1980. Even in this country, though, there are no grounds for complacency.

For one thing, present inflation is low partly because of the long and persistent overvaluation of the U.S. dollar. The strong dollar of the 1979–84 period allowed us to buy an enormous amount of imports at reduced prices. If the dollar were properly aligned with other major trading currencies, our inflation rate would probably be three full percentage points higher—nearly 5 percent.

Currency alignments are never static. In the early '70s, as today, the U.S. dollar was dramatically overvalued. In 1970 the Swiss franc stood at 4.32 francs to the dollar. Nine years later the ratio was 1.58 francs to the dollar. The dollar fell by over 60 percent in nine years.

When the dollar decline of 1985–86 feeds completely into the system, we can expect a return to 5 percent inflation based on that factor alone.

But that's not all. The enormous rise in the U.S. budget deficit must also lead, over the long run, to higher inflation. When a government borrows money at the rate the U.S. government borrows money, it is vital that future interest payments on that debt—and principal amounts, if any—be made with cheaper dollars, not more expensive dollars. This is the primary reason why inflation tends to win out over deflation over the long term.

"Do as I Say, Not as I Do"

In November 1980, Ronald Reagan was elected President. He was swept into office on a tide of conservative rhetoric—a tight-fisted budget balancer if there ever was one.

Let's see how things have gone.

At the end of 1980, total gross federal debt stood at $928 billion. In the ensuing four years, the Republican administration dug in its heels and preached fiscal responsibility. Four years later, at the end of 1984, total gross federal debt stood at $1,660 billion. That is, during President Reagan's first term, the U.S. debt had been allowed to expand by $732 billion. In only four years the "conservative" administration had practically doubled the nation's federal debt.

It is hard to imagine less conservative results from even the most freewheeling of liberal Democrats. At least with a Democrat regime, there is some opposition from the Republicans.

During his first term of office, President Reagan presided over a buildup in debt that equals a 15.7 percent compound growth rate. At 15.7 percent, money (or debt) doubles in only five years and triples in eight years. And the situation had become worse, not better, during the course of Reagan's first term. From June 1982 through June 1984, federal debt ballooned from $1,098 billion to $1,526 billion—an expansion of the debt that was nearly as great as the *total* debt of $447 billion in 1972. That represented a compound growth rate of 18.4 percent. At that rate, money doubles in just over four years and triples in six-and-a-half years.

As the Federal Reserve reported in 1985, "the rise in domestic nonfinancial debt recorded in 1984 was *the largest on record in the postwar period.* Federal government debt continued to show the fastest growth, but borrowing by other sectors [households, businesses, local and state governments] was substantial as well."

Despite all the rhetoric from Capitol Hill and the White House, this distressing trend shows no sign of reversal. By

March 1986, the federal debt had jumped to $1,993 billion. And, as I write, the debt projection for March 1987 is $2,310 billion—*over two trillion dollars!*

The Ominous Change in the Budget Deficit

Before the Reagan administration, the biggest increases in the federal deficit came during recessions. That's not too surprising. In a recession, receipts from taxes fall due to the economic contraction. Uncle Sam's expenditures do not fall, however. Spending goes on as planned and like clockwork. The difference between the falling receipts and rising expenditures is reflected in a rising deficit.

Now, however, the federal deficit is increasing even in times of rapid economic expansion. This is a most serious development, a signal that spending is out of control.

During the 1973–75 recession, the three-year budget deficit was approximately $65 billion. During this period, expenditures advanced 63 percent ahead of receipts. The negative impact of recession slowed receipts, but did little to halt the government's addiction to spending.

During the 1980–82 recession, the budget deficit totalled approximately $229 billion—about four times the 1973–75 deficit. During this period, outlays advanced over receipts by nearly 50 percent. The same pattern prevailed as in the previous recession: Receipts slowed, but spending moved on at an ever-increasing rate of speed.

The years 1983–85 were ones of economic recovery and expansion. Yet in those years the budget deficit totalled approximately $754 billion. Even with the expansion, federal expenditures advanced approximately 50 percent faster than federal receipts.

If we are going into the hole this rapidly in a time of great expansion, what will happen during the next recession? Well, if you listen to some of the most prominent Republican leaders, they have repealed the business cycle. You won't find a hint of recession in any of their projections.

If you don't buy that, what can you expect? During the recessionary year of 1982, receipts declined by 2.2 percent from the previous year's level. As I write, the government has projected receipts of $777 billion and expenditures of $980 billion for Fiscal 1986, for a deficit of $203 billion; and receipts of $850 billion and expenditures of $994 billion for Fiscal 1987, for a deficit that year of $144 billion. That's counting on a lot of growth in receipts—from $777 billion to $850 billion. If, however, there is a recession similar to the one in 1982, receipts for 1987 would decline (by 2.2 percent) to $760 billion rather than increase to $850 billion, and this $90 billion difference would increase the deficit in 1987 to $234 billion.

And it was just yesterday that we were shocked at the prospect of a $100 billion budget deficit.

Where Will It All End?

• The last internal budget surplus was recorded in 1969. Today the United States features a triple-digit internal budget deficit.

• The last trade surplus was recorded in 1975. Today the United States features a triple-digit external trade deficit.

• In 1984, the combined external/internal deficit exceeded $300 billion for the first time in history.

Where will the money come from to finance deficits of such enormity? There are only three possibilities:

The first is a foreign bailout. But that's only a theoretical possibility. What foreign country has the surplus wealth to bail the United States out of such deficits?

That leaves two options: We pay today, or we pay tomorrow. And which option will the politicians choose? No problem with that one—take the medicine tomorrow.

Paying today would mean cutting the federal deficit rather than expanding it. That, in turn, would require drastically higher taxes and/or drastic cuts in government expenditures, and those are not ways politicians get re-elected. If, on the other hand, the government went into the bond market to balance the books, it would be competing with industry for the available pool of capital. The result would be a new wave of interest rate hikes.

The clear route is the *currently* painless one of printing new money that is not presently in the pool of available capital. Print new money and pay off the debt—or at least service it—in cheaper dollars tomorrow.

Thus, there can be little doubt that as long as massive deficits persist, money supply growth will be excessive. That, in turn, points to inflation. Far from being dead, inflation is a very real threat—*over the long run*—that the prudent investor must take into account.

The Banking Crisis

As you read this, the banking system is more highly leveraged than at any previous point in your lifetime—no matter what your age. As a result of this shrinking liquidity, the banking system is increasingly subject to financial shocks.

What is bank liquidity? It's the percentage of total bank credit (loans and investments) held in liquid portfolio investments such as U.S. Treasury securities. The lower the amount of liquidity, the less likelihood there is that the bank could survive massive loan defaults or a major run on deposits.

We have liquidity figures going back to the establishment of the Federal Reserve System in 1913. During the early days and up to the Great Depression, liquidity tended to hold at around 30 percent.

During the Great Depression and World War II, liquidity steadily improved. A peak reading of 63 percent was recorded in 1950.

By 1960, bank liquidity had been reduced to 40 percent. By 1971, to 31 percent. By 1980, to 21 percent. And by December 1985, to 17 percent.

A day of reckoning must arrive. Liquidity cannot fall to zero. Yet, at the current rate of decline, liquidity will reach the zero level by the end of the decade.

International liquidity is following the same path. In 1950, one dollar of central bank foreign exchange reserves was backed by three dollars in gold. Today the ratio has fallen to one-to-one.

As I have already mentioned, this shrinking liquidity makes the banking system increasingly subject to financial shocks. And financial shocks are becoming increasingly probable. The most obvious threat is massive defaults of Third World debts.

We have already seen how Central and South American countries are being ravaged by inflation. This inflation threatens their ability to pay the interest on their enormous bank debts, much less pay off the principal. Just as serious a threat of default, however, comes from Africa.

We can see this from data published by the International Monetary Fund. The fund is a lender, but unlike commercial banks, it does not roll over bad debts, and unlike most governments, it actually has a limit on how much it will lend anyone. Quotas are established and, in theory at least, no country is allowed to borrow more than 450 percent of its quota.

When examining the tables on who has been borrowing, how often, and how much, we find that no industrialized country is in even the slightest jam. Central and South America, however, are a different story. Bearing in mind that 450 percent is the limit on loans, we find that Argentina (224 percent), Brazil (273 percent), Dominica (211 percent), Ecuador (231 percent), Panama (265 percent), Jamaica (415 percent), and Mexico (253 percent) are all borrowing with a vengeance.

As dismaying as these figures are, more hot spots are in Africa. The following countries are fast approaching the point (450 percent) where the financial faucet theoretically is shut off: Kenya (283 percent), Liberia (288 percent), Malawi (303 percent), Mauritius (254 percent), Morocco (310 percent), Somalia (280 percent), Sudan (357 percent), Uganda (217 percent), and Zambia (259 percent).

Elsewhere in the world, we find South Korea (296 percent), Thailand (215 percent), and Yugoslavia (306 percent) deeply in debt. But these are a few individual countries, while the entire continents of Africa and South America are in trouble. For the developing countries in Africa, as a whole, the debt figures have risen from 47 percent in 1979 to 105 percent in mid-1986. For the South American countries as a whole, the debt figures have risen from 31 percent in 1979 to 170 percent in mid-1986.

As I've noted, this explosion in borrowings in most cases did not take place during the oil crises of the 1970s but *since* the late '70s. World debt is a time bomb that continues to tick below the surface of the current illusion of financial stability.

Yes, I Worry!

• Worldwide inflation remains a serious threat to the world economy and is no longer tied to oil price jumps.

• U.S. spending appears to be headed out of control, with massive deficits increasing in years of prosperity as well as in periods of recession.

• And a world banking crisis is increasingly possible, thanks to the erosion of bank liquidity.

Yes, I worry!

I'm not exactly losing sleep over these problems, however. For one thing, I've learned that the world's economy is much too complicated to be predictable with any certainty. Trends never follow a straight line in any direction, and that's why the world is still functioning, however imperfectly. For another thing, I've learned how to diversify my investments so that I come out ahead no matter which way the world turns. And that's the best sleeping pill imaginable!

But how about you? If you have been basking in Reaganite complacency, I hope I have caught your attention. Now let's see what we can do to protect *your* assets from these very possible, if not inevitable, catastrophes.

· TWO ·

U.S. Treasury Securities

U.S. Treasury bills (T-bills) and notes are one of the safest investments you can make, for the reasons I gave in the Introduction. But can you also make a decent return on them?

Harry Browne, a noted investment author and advisor, has tracked the record of twenty different investments for the five years 1980 through 1984. He found that "U.S. Treasury bills outperformed every investment but one for the five-year period." T-bills brought a 76.3 percent gain over that period, but were edged out of first place by gold stocks, which gained 78.3 percent. (Stock mutual funds, not counted among the twenty individual types of investments, gave a 96.3 percent return over those five years, and the Consumer Price Index jumped 37.2 percent.)

While gold stocks did slightly better than T-bills over the entire 1980–84 period, there was a vital difference. T-bills brought a solid return *every year*. Gold stocks, on the other hand, gave what Harry Browne called "a roller coaster performance." Twice they were among the year's top five investments, and two other years they were among the five worst.

When looking at the performance of different investments, of course, the past is not necessarily prologue. You have to use the knowledge and techniques I give you in this book to keep your portfolio constantly updated. I gave you this recent history, though, so you can see that Treasury securities are not automatically poor investments in terms of their return. When the times are right, Treasury securities can bring you bedrock safety *and* decent profits.

In Chapter 5, I will show you how to decide exactly which

Treasury securities to buy, and how much to buy in relation to gold. Here, in this chapter, I will show you *how* to buy them.

A Note About Treasury Bonds

When I talk about buying Treasury securities, I am referring to Treasury bills and notes. I specifically exclude Treasury bonds.

What is the key difference between these three types of Treasury securities? Their maturities. *Bills* mature in three months (thirteen weeks), six months (twenty-six weeks), or one year (fifty-two weeks). *Notes* mature in one to ten years. *Bonds* mature in more than ten years, and up to thirty years.

And why do I exclude bonds from my portfolio? Because they add a great amount of risk with no necessary corresponding increase in profits. Over a long period of time, inflation can wipe out your fixed rate of return. The current rates of return on Treasury securities, moreover, increase as you go from short-term T-bills to medium-term T-notes, but then are relatively flat after seven years. That is why I limit my purchases to Treasury bills and notes, generally with maturities of up to seven years.

How to Play the Millionaire's Game
on *Your* Terms

Once upon a time, Treasury securities were the exclusive province of the investment market's big players—banks, institutions, funds, and individual millionaires. That's not surprising when you consider that traditionally $1 million has been the minimum normal trading unit for Treasury securities. Even today, anything less than $1 million is considered an "odd lot."

So, how can you hope to play this game? It's easy, thanks to the changes in the financial market that have taken place in recent years. The growth of mutual funds, money market funds, and individual retirement accounts (IRAs) has expanded to include Treasury securities, and later in this chapter I will give my recommendations on how and where to buy Treasury securities in that way.

But you can also buy individual Treasury notes for as little as $1,000 and individual Treasury bills for a minimum of $10,000. Uncle Sam, in his desperate bid for funds to finance his ever-growing deficits, has noticed that there are many more investors who can afford $1,000 units than investors who can afford $1 million units, and he has made it *easy* for you to loan him the money in those amounts. A significant portion of Treasury securities is now bought by smaller individual investors such as you.

There are three basic ways you can buy Treasury securities as individual units—through your bank or thrift association, through your broker, or directly from the U.S. Treasury through your local Federal Reserve bank. There are two reasons why I suggest you buy directly from Uncle Sam.

Fees are the first reason. You pay no fee when buying directly from a Federal Reserve bank, but brokerage and financial institutions will charge you a fee that may range between $25 and $50.

That may not appear to be a significant difference, but the more important difference is the total price (including fee) you pay for your security. Remember that the normal trading unit for Treasury securities is still $1 million. In trader's language, that normal trading unit of $1 million is called a "round lot" and anything less than $1 million is called an "odd lot." For the inconvenience of dealing in such piddling amounts, brokers will make you pay more to buy an odd lot and they will pay you less when you want to sell an odd lot. Exactly how they determine their prices is often clothed in secrecy and considered proprietary information. This secrecy, of course, makes it virtually impossible for you to do comparison shopping.

The smaller the amounts you buy, the bigger the difference this makes, because you are paying the broker's minimum fee for each transaction. If you buy $100,000 in Treasury securities at a time, you may find it worth the convenience to do your buying and selling through a broker. But for a $1,000 order of two-year notes, the broker's higher price could reduce your yield by one and a half percentage points—and that's significant.

When you buy your Treasury securities directly through a Federal Reserve bank, you pay no odd-lot fee. You pay the *average* price of what the big players are paying. Yes, some of them are paying slightly less than you, but it should make you feel good to know that the other half of these giant, sophisticated traders are paying more than you!

Here's how it works.

The price paid for Treasury securities—and thus the investment yield you get from them—is determined by auction. Uncle Sam doesn't set the price; the buyers do. That's why the yield on Treasury securities rises with inflation—or even the threat of rising inflation. The buyers (investors) want to make certain they get a real return, taking inflation into account.

There are two ways to bid for a Treasury security. You can submit a *competitive* bid or a *noncompetitive* bid.

Competitive bids must specify not only the amount of the securities they want to purchase but also the price or yield that they are willing to pay. This requires a great deal of skill and detailed, up-to-the-minute knowledge of financial trends. That's why most competitive bidders are money market banks, dealers, and other institutional investors who regularly buy large quantities of Treasury securities.

Small bidders or inexperienced investors are usually better off submitting a noncompetitive bid. With a noncompetitive bid, you are not required to state a price or yield. You simply indicate the amount of securities you wish to purchase, and agree to accept the *average* price or yield established in the auction. This protects you from the risk of paying more than the going market price, and it assures you that your bid will be accepted within certain limitations.

After the auction for a new security, the Treasury first totals all noncompetitive bids. If it wants to sell, say, $2.5 billion of the new issue and it gets $500 million in noncompetitive bids, it knows it has $2 billion left to sell to the competitive bidders. It allocates this beginning with those that bid the highest prices and ranging down in price until the total amount is issued. The lowest accepted price is called the *stop-out* price. Noncompetitive bids are then awarded at the average price of all the accepted competitive bids.

In summary, for most smaller investors the best way to buy Treasury securities is to buy them directly from the Federal Reserve bank for your region, and by submitting a noncompetitive bid. In this way, you pay no fees and you are protected from the risk of paying more than the going market price for the securities.

Now let's see how you do this.

How to Buy Treasury Bills Directly
from Uncle Sam

Treasury bills (T-bills) are short-term securities issued with maturities of thirteen weeks, twenty-six weeks, and fifty-two weeks respectively. They are sold in minimum amounts of $10,000, and in multiples of $5,000 above the minimum.

Treasury bills are issued only in book-entry form. In effect, this means that purchasers receive a receipt rather than an engraved certificate as evidence of their purchase. Your ownership is recorded in a book-entry account established for purchasers at the Treasury, and this protects you against loss, theft, and counterfeiting.

T-bills are not redeemable at the Treasury before maturity. At any time, though, you can buy or sell already-issued Treasury bills through financial institutions, brokers, and dealers in investment securities. You pay them a premium for this service, as I've noted, but it is comforting to know that you have this liquidity if you need it.

Here are answers to some questions you may have about buying Treasury bills.

Where Can I Purchase Treasury Bills?

You can purchase them directly from the Treasury in Washington, D.C., or (preferably) from the Federal Reserve bank or branch for your region. Table 3 lists these, with their addresses and telephone numbers. If you are not certain which Federal Reserve bank serves your area, ask your local commercial banker.

When Are New Treasury Bills Offered?

Two series of bills, those with thirteen-week maturities and those with twenty-six week maturities, are offered each week. The pattern for these weekly issues is as follows:

1. The offering is announced on Tuesday.
2. The bills are auctioned the following Monday.
3. The bills are issued on the Thursday after the auction.

Treasury bills with fifty-two week maturities are also offered every four weeks, as follows:

1. The offering is announced every fourth Friday (for the exact date contact your local Federal Reserve bank).
2. The bills are auctioned the following Thursday.
3. The bills are issued on the following Thursday.

When a normal auction date falls on a holiday, the auction is usually held on the preceding business day. Announcements of forthcoming auctions are printed in the financial pages of major newspapers, or you can call your local Federal Reserve bank for information about forthcoming issues.

When Can I Purchase New Treasury Bills?

You must submit a tender—a bid—before the auction.

If you do this in person, you must go to the Federal Reserve bank or branch between 9 A.M. and 2 P.M. on a business day before the auction, or before 1:30 P.M. on the day of the auction.

If you submit your bid by mail, it must also be received by the Federal Reserve bank or branch no later than 1:30 P.M. on the day of the auction.

If you submit your bid directly to the Treasury, it must be postmarked no later than midnight of the prior day and received no later than the date of issue. (Normally, this requires mailing during the week before the auction.)

Any tender received after the deadline is automatically held for the next auction, unless you specifically request that it be returned.

How Do I Submit a Tender?

You can call or write your local Federal Reserve bank and ask for the special forms on which to submit a tender for Treasury bills. Alternatively, you can submit a letter rather than a tender form. Just be sure to type or print it carefully and to include the following information:

1. The face amount of the bills requested.

2. The maturity desired (thirteen, twenty-six, or fifty-two weeks).

3. Whether you are submitting a noncompetitive or competitive bid, and if competitive, the price.

4. Whether you want to reinvest the funds at maturity.

5. The account identification, which includes your name and mailing address (for co-ownership, the first name of your spouse must be included).

6. Your social security number (two social security numbers are required for co-ownership).

7. Your telephone number during business hours.

8. Your signature.

Your tender and payment should be mailed to the attention of the Fiscal Agency Department of the Federal Reserve bank or branch in your area (see Table 3). At the bottom of the envelope, print or type the words "Tender for Treasury Bills."

How Do I Pay for New Bills?

Payment for the full face value of the Treasury bill must accompany the tender. Your payment can be made in one of the following forms:

1. In U.S. currency (not recommended for submissions by mail)

2. By certified personal check

3. By check issued by a commercial bank, savings and loan association, savings bank, or credit union (provided such checks are drawn to the order of a specified Federal Reserve bank or the U.S. Treasury)

4. With redemption checks issued by the Bureau of Public Debt in payment of matured Treasury bills, provided the tender is submitted in the name(s) of the payee(s)

5. In matured U.S. Treasury securities (notes or bonds).

How Much Will I End Up Paying for the Treasury Bills?

Since your bid must be submitted before the auction (which is not open to observers), you will never know the auction results or your return in advance. You can get a general idea of what the cost is likely to be—and thus the return on your investment—by looking at the results of recent auctions.

The Treasury usually announces the result of the auction the day afterwards. The *Wall Street Journal* and major local newspapers carry these announcements, or you can call your local Federal Reserve bank for the information.

As already noted, your initial check must be for the full face amount of the bill. When the issue price is determined by the auction, the Treasury will send you a check for the difference. For example, if the price of a $10,000 bill turns out to be $9,850, the Treasury will send you a refund check for $150. This check is a *refund,* though, and not prepaid interest.

How Can I Determine the Investment Yield on My Treasury Bill?

You buy a Treasury bill at a price below its face value, called its discount price. When it matures, you redeem the bill at its face value. If you hold the bill to maturity, the difference between the purchase price (discount price) and face value represents your earnings. You are familiar with this process if you have ever bought a U.S. savings bond.

These earnings are often expressed not as a dollar amount, but as a rate of return. It is important for you to distinguish between two different types of rates of return. The *discount rate* is based on the full face value (say, $10,000) of the bill. The *investment yield* is based on your actual purchase price of the bill. The investment yield is what you want to use to compare your earnings or rate of return from the Treasury bill with your earnings or rate of return from other investments.

Most newspapers report both the discount rate and the investment yield for Treasury securities. Let's assume an auction has just been held, though, and the only information you have is that the discount rate for a twenty-six-week Treasury bill you purchased is 10.875 percent.

Here is how you determine what your investment yield will be.

First, compute the dollar amount of your earnings, using this formula:

Discount rate × face value of the bill

$$\times \frac{\text{Days to maturity}}{365^*} = \text{earnings.}$$

In this example, the figures would be as follows:

$$10.875\% \times \$10,000 \times \frac{182 \text{ days (26 weeks)}}{365} = \text{earnings.}$$

$$\$1,087.50 \times .4986 = \$542.23 \text{ (or approximately \$542).}$$

You can soon expect a refund check of $542 from the Treasury, meaning that you paid $9,458 for your Treasury bill.

Second, to translate your dollar earnings figure ($542) into an investment yield, use this formula:

$$\frac{\text{earnings (in dollars)}}{\text{price paid for bill}} \times \frac{\text{number of days in year}}{\text{days to bill's maturity}} =$$

$$\frac{542}{9458} \times \frac{365}{182} = .0573 \times 2.0055 = 0.1149 \ (11.5\%)$$

You now know that your Treasury bill will bring you an investment yield of 11.5 percent if you hold it to maturity, and you can compare this yield with the yield you are getting from your other investments. I repeat, however, that in most instances you will not have to do this mathematical figuring, since most newspaper reports give both the discount rate and the investment yield.

How to Buy Treasury Notes
Directly from Uncle Sam

Treasury notes have a maturity of not less than one year and not more than ten years from the date of issue. Notes maturing in four years or longer are usually offered in a minimum denomination of $1,000. Notes maturing in less than four years are usually offered in a minimum denomination of $5,000, and purchases may be made in any higher multiples of $5,000.

Procedures for buying Treasury notes are pretty much the

---

*Number of days in a year; use 366 in leap years.

same as for buying Treasury bills. Here are some differences, though.

Schedule for Sales

In recent years, the usual pattern has been as follows:

Two-year notes are issued at the end of each month.

Four-year notes are issued in March, June, September, and December.

Five-year notes are issued in January, July, and October.

Other securities—usually including a three-to-five-year note and a seven-to-ten-year note—are offered every three months during the Treasury's quarterly financings, on the fifteenth of February, May, August, and November.

Announcements of these auctions appear in the financial sections of major newspapers a week or two before the sales. You may also call your local Federal Reserve bank (see Table 3) for information about forthcoming note offerings.

Deadline for Tenders

Noncompetitive tenders are accepted even if received after the deadline, provided they are postmarked no later than the day prior to the auction.

Form of Payment

This is the same as for Treasury bills, except that you may send a personal check or mutual fund check that is not certified.

Investment Yield

Treasury notes pay a fixed interest rate. The interest earnings are paid to you twice a year, or every six months. The security itself may be redeemed at maturity for its face value. (As with Treasury bills, you may sell notes before they mature through a broker or other financial institution.)

When you submit payment for your tender, it must be for the face value of the note. The actual purchase price is determined by the auction, however, and if you submit a noncompetitive tender you pay the average price of the accepted competitive bids. This may be less or more than the face value of the note. Accordingly, you will be mailed a refund or required to pay the additional amount. If a $1,000 note sells *above par*, for example, that means its purchase price is more than $1,000. If it sells *below par*, its purchase price is less than $1,000.

Your *annual return* is equal to the face value of the security times the interest rate. For example, a $1,000 note with an interest rate of 12 percent returns $120 a year ($1,000 × .12).

Your *investment yield* will be somewhat different, however, depending on the purchase price of the note. If the purchase price was below par (below the face value), the investment yield will be greater than the interest rate. If the purchase price was above par, the investment yield will be less than the interest rate.

When Treasury notes are auctioned, the results are printed in the financial sections of major newspapers and include the investment yield.

How to Use Treasury Securities as Collateral

The Treasury will not get involved in helping you pledge Treasury bills as collateral. It will not recognize a pledge of book-entry securities for collateral, nor will it transfer securities among book-entry accounts that it maintains.

There is a way to work this out with your commercial bank, however. Let's say you own a $10,000 Treasury bill on a book-entry account and want to pledge it as collateral for a loan from a bank. First, request Form PD 4633 from your local Federal Reserve bank. Then, in the section marked "Action Requested," request the transfer of your Treasury bill from your book-entry account at the Treasury to the account of the commercial bank (member bank) held at a regional Federal Reserve bank.

Once this transfer is complete, the Treasury bill is no longer yours; it is the property of the commercial bank. You must have the bank's written verification, therefore, that $10,000 of the Treasury bills held in its account at the Federal Reserve bank constitutes collateral for your loan. When you pay off your loan and the bill matures, the bank then credits your checking account for $10,000.

A Note About Trading Treasury Securities

My advice in this book is given with your long-term investment security and gain in mind. In most instances, therefore, I suggest that you purchase your Treasury securities and hold them until maturity.

Some traders seek profits by speculating on interest rate moves. This requires considerable expertise, however, and at any rate should not be attempted by buying odd lots of Treasury securities. T-bill and T-note futures markets are much cheaper ways to do that.

Where to Get Further Information on Buying Treasury Securities

Most Federal Reserve banks have publications to help you understand Treasury securities. Single copies are free, and you do not have to reside in a bank's district to order these publications. See Table 3 for the addresses of these Federal Reserve banks. Here are some publications that are particularly useful.

From the Federal Reserve Bank of Richmond

"Buying Treasury Securities at Federal Reserve Banks," by James F. Tucker. This is the most useful and comprehensive publication on this subject.

From the Federal Reserve Bank of New York

"Basic Information on Treasury Bills."
   "Basic Information on Treasury Notes and Bonds."
   "The Arithmetic of Interest Rates" (how to compute returns on Treasury issues).
   "Federal Reserve System Public Information Materials" (detailed bibliography of publications and periodicals available from the Federal Reserve banks).

From the Federal Reserve Bank of Dallas

"United States Treasury Securities—Basic Information." (The appeal of this publication is its topical arrangement in three columns—for bills, notes, and bonds.)

Investing in Treasury Securities
Through a Mutual Fund, IRA, or Keogh

I mentioned earlier in this chapter that an easy way to invest in Treasury securities is through a money market mutual fund, an individual retirement account (IRA), or a Keogh retirement plan. My favorite company providing these services for investors in Treasury securities is Benham Capital Management Group of Palo Alto, California.

This "family" of government securities funds was conceived by James M. Benham in 1970 as a new kind of investment vehicle, one that would invest in U.S. Treasury securities to enable the public to keep up with the inflation rate he predicted would spiral upward in the 1970s. The group's first fund—the Capital Preservation Fund—was started in 1972, making it the nation's second oldest money market fund and the first one to concentrate its portfolio in Treasury securities. Today it manages more than $2.5 billion for over 150,000 investors, making it also the largest Treasury-invested money market fund in existence.

The primary objective of the Capital Preservation Fund is maximum safety and liquidity. Its secondary objective is the highest rate of return consistent with that safety and liquidity. Accordingly, it invests *exclusively and directly* in short-term (one year or less) U.S. Treasury bills. These are the *only* investments the fund makes. Unlike many other money market funds, it does not invest in certificates of deposit from banks and savings and loans, corporate debt securities, or securities issued by agencies of the federal government.

While neither this fund, nor any other money market fund, is insured or backed by the government, the fact that it invests only in U.S. Treasury securities means that the full taxing power of the government stands behind Uncle Sam's promise to redeem the fund's portfolio securities at maturity, no matter what happens to the money and credit markets. It is relevant to note that, nationwide, FDIC and FSLIC "insurance" is a pool of about $19.0 billion, backing over $1.5 trillion in deposits in federally chartered banks and thrifts. And where is this pool of money invested? In Treasury securities, the same as with the Capital Preservation Fund.

Another plus I have found is that the fund's monthly statements are excellent. The information presented in them is easy to read and comprehend.

You can invest in the fund without paying any fees or commissions. The minimum initial investment is $1,000, and additional investments may be made in amounts of $100 or more.

Another member of Benham's "family" of funds is the Capital Preservation Treasury Note Trust. It differs from Capital Preservation Fund in that it invests at least 90 percent of its portfolio in Treasury *notes*, which, as we've seen, provide a higher return than short-term bills. The Trust may invest the remaining 10 percent of its assets in U.S. Treasury bills and repurchase agreements consisting of U.S. Treasury securities.

State Income Taxes

Treasury securities that you buy directly are exempt from state and local income taxes. This is not necessarily the case, however, with income received from money market funds, even a fund that invests solely in Treasury securities.

The Benham officers have been waging a valiant fight against state and local taxation, arguing that there should be no difference in tax treatment when the money market fund invests exclusively in U.S. Treasury securities. You should check with your tax advisor or state tax officials. Currently, though, the following states say they agree with Benham and will not tax dividends a resident receives from the Capital Preservation Fund: Alabama, Arizona, Colorado, District of Columbia, Georgia, Hawaii, Idaho, Kansas, Louisiana, Maine, Montana, Nebraska, North Carolina, Utah, and Virginia.

Tax-Deferred Retirement Plans

Both IRA and Keogh plans are available for Benham investors. I discuss these types of retirement plans in detail in Chapter 13.

Under a Keogh plan, self-employed persons may make federally tax-deductible investments in a fund (such as these Benham funds) of up to $30,000 or 20 percent of their earned income each year (whichever is less). All income earned on the investment accumulates tax-free until withdrawal, which normally begins at retirement. Because Keogh plan contributions are deductible from gross income in computing adjusted gross income, investors enjoy full tax-deferred benefits even when they take the "standard deduction."

With an individual retirement account (IRA), you currently can invest and deduct from gross income up to $2,000 or 100 percent of your earned income, whichever is less, each year. All income earned on the investment accumulates tax-free until withdrawal, which again normally begins at retirement.

As this book goes to press, the 1986 tax bill proposes major changes in IRA tax treatment, but that bill is still pending before Congress. See Chapter 13 for details.

For Further Information on the Benham Group

You may get further information from the Benham Capital Management Group, 755 Page Mill Road, P.O. Box 10125, Palo Alto, CA 94303-9968. Telephone (415) 858-2400 or use one of the following toll-free numbers. From all states: (800) 472-3389 or (800) 4-SAFETY. From California: (800) 982-6150. From other mainland states: (800) 227-8380. From Alaska and Hawaii: (800) 848-0002.

TABLE 3
Federal Reserve Banks and U.S. Treasury
Addresses and Telephone Numbers

Federal Reserve Bank of Boston	Address (mark envelope "Attention: Fiscal Agency Dept.") 600 Atlantic Avenue, Boston, MA 02106 (617) 973-3800

New York	33 Liberty Street (Federal Reserve P.O. Station), New York, NY 10045 (212) 791-5823 (Telephone 24 hours a day, including Saturday and Sunday)
Buffalo branch	160 Delaware Avenue (P.O. Box 961), Buffalo, NY 14240 (716) 849-5046
Philadelphia	100 North Sixth Street (P.O. Box 90), Philadelphia, PA 19105 (215) 574-6580
Cleveland	1455 East Sixth Street (P.O. Box 6387), Cleveland, OH 44101 (216) 579-2490
Cincinnati branch	150 East Fourth Street (P.O. Box 999), Cincinnati, OH 45201 (513) 721-4787, ext. 332
Pittsburgh branch	717 Grant Street (P.O. Box 867), Pittsburgh, PA 15230 (412) 261-7864
Richmond	701 East Byrd Street (P.O. Box 27622), Richmond, VA 23261 (804) 643-1250
Baltimore branch	114-120 East Lexington Street (P.O. Box 1378), Baltimore, MD 21203 (301) 576-3300
Charlotte branch	401 South Tryon Street (P.O. Box 30248), Charlotte, NC 28230 (704) 373-0200
Atlanta	104 Marietta Street, N.W. (P.O. Box 1731), Atlanta, GA 30301 (404) 586-8657

Birmingham branch	1801 Fifth Avenue, North (P.O. Box 10447), Birmingham, AL 35202 (205) 252-3141, ext. 215
Jacksonville branch	515 Julia Street, Jacksonville, FL 32231 (904) 354-8211, ext. 211
Miami branch	3770 S.W. 8th Street, Coral Gables, FL 33134 (P.O. Box 847), Miami, FL 33152 (305) 591-2065
Nashville branch	301 Eighth Avenue, North, Nashville, TN 37203 (615) 259-4006
New Orleans branch	525 St. Charles Avenue (P.O. Box 61630), New Orleans, LA 70161 (504) 586-1505, ext. 230, 240, 242
Chicago	230 South LaSalle Street (P.O. Box 834), Chicago, IL 60690 (312) 786-1110
Detroit branch	160 Fort Street, West (P.O. Box 1059), Detroit, MI 48231 (313) 961-6880, ext. 372, 373
St. Louis	411 Locust Street (P.O. Box 442), St. Louis, MO 63166 (314) 444-8444
Little Rock branch	325 West Capitol Avenue (P.O. Box 1261), Little Rock, AR 72203 (501) 372-5451, ext. 270
Louisville branch	410 South Fifth Street (P.O. Box 899), Louisville, KY 40201 (502) 587-7351, ext. 237, 301

Memphis branch	200 North Main Street (P.O. Box 407), Memphis, TN 38101 (901) 523-7171
Minneapolis	250 Marquette Avenue, Minneapolis, MN 55480 (612) 340-2051
Helena branch	400 North Park Avenue, Helena, MT 59601 (406) 442-3860
Kansas City	925 Grand Avenue (Federal Reserve Station), Kansas City, MO 64198 (816) 881-2783
Denver branch	1020 16th Street (P.O. Box 5228, Terminal Annex), Denver, CO 80217 (303) 292-4020
Oklahoma City branch	226 Northwest Third Street (P.O. Box 25129), Oklahoma City, OK 73125 (405) 235-1721, ext. 182
Omaha branch	102 South Seventeenth Street, Omaha, NE 68102 (402) 341-3610, ext. 242
Dallas	400 South Akard Street (Station K), Dallas, TX 75222 (214) 651-6177
El Paso branch	301 East Main Street (P.O. Box 100), El Paso, TX 79999 (915) 544-4730, ext. 57
Houston branch	1701 San Jacinto Street (P.O. Box 2578), Houston, TX 77001 (713) 659-4433, ext. 19, 74, 75, 76
San Antonio branch	126 East Nueva Street (P.O. Box 1471), San Antonio, TX 78295 (512) 224-2141, ext. 61, 66

San Francisco	400 Sansome Street (P.O. Box 7702), San Francisco, CA 94120 (415) 392-6639
Los Angeles branch	409 West Olympic Boulevard (P.O. Box 2077, Terminal Annex), Los Angeles, CA 90051 (213) 683-8563
Portland branch	915 S.W. Stark Street (P.O. Box 3436), Portland, OR 97208 (503) 228-7584
Salt Lake City branch	120 South State Street (P.O. Box 30780), Salt Lake City, UT 84127 (801) 355-3131, ext. 251, 270
Seattle branch	1015 Second Avenue (P.O. Box 3567), Seattle, WA 98124 (206) 442-1650

Treasury *General information and application for new bills*	Bureau of the Public Debt, Securities Transactions Branch, Main Treasury Building, Room 2134, Washington, DC 20226 (202) 566-2604
Specific account information and transaction requests	Bureau of the Public Debt, Public-Entry, Washington, DC 20226 (202) 634-5487

· THREE ·

Gold

It is easy to fall in love with gold. The yellow metal, a universal symbol of wealth, has enthralled people since the dawn of civilization.

There are solid, irrefutable reasons why gold should be a part of most investors' portfolios. But precisely because it *is* so alluring, the intelligent investor also needs unemotional, rational benchmarks to use as guides when investing in gold.

It is just as critical to know *how* to invest in gold; the waters are full of sharks.

Finally, it is also essential to keep gold's short-term fluctuations and cycles in perspective. In a free market, gold's price tends to rise and fall with the rate of inflation. That's why its performance can be so lackluster in periods of low inflation or disinflation, such as the past few years. Over the long run, though, no other form of money holds its value as well as gold.

The Allure of Gold

In ancient Greece, gold was considered divine. It adorned temples and was used in offerings to the gods. At the same time, why should the gods get all of a good thing? Gold's malleability made it ideal for jewelry, and Cleopatra established herself as a role model for countless future vamps by enhancing her physical charms with gold ornaments.

Even myths probably had some basis in what we'd today call "the facts." The legendary "golden fleece" sought by Jason, for example, may have been nothing more than a sheepskin used to remove tiny grains of gold from streams.

Throughout history, the quest for gold shifted nations' borders and opened wildernesses. "Get gold," King Ferdinand commanded Spain's soldiers in South America, "humanely if possible, but at all hazards get gold."

Gold as Money

The earliest gold coins known to history were cast around 550 B.C., probably by King Croesus of Lydia (now western Turkey). However, payments in gold had already been made for hundreds of years. The coin format merely made the transactions easier and more exact.

If we took a poll of present-day Americans, most probably would define "money" as the paper bills and change in their pockets, their deposits in a bank or financial institution, and perhaps their line of credit with various credit cards. Relatively few would mention gold. Yet, looked at historically, this is an amazingly parochial viewpoint, for, throughout history, gold has been the most common, universal, and persistent form of money.

Why?

Gold's *beauty* is only a beginning. Its *malleability* is certainly a consideration, especially when making coins (or jewelry, which can also be used as money in times of distress). Certainly the fact that gold is virtually *indestructible* is a plus—King Tut's treasures are still bright after three thousand years.

Most important, however, is gold's *scarcity*. All the gold ever mined since the beginning of time could fit into a cube nineteen yards per side. The weight of this cube—roughly one hundred thousand tons—would be no more than the amount of metal the American steel industry pours in about five hours.

Why is this scarcity so important? Because it makes gold an ideal store of value. You can't create more gold by digging in your back yard, or by turning on the printing press. As we will see in Chapter 10 ("What the Financial Armadillo Must Know About Inflation"), this is the problem with paper money. When governments print more paper money without a corresponding increase in productivity, the result is monetary inflation, followed by price inflation. They just can't do that with gold. *This makes gold your premier protection against inflation and other forms of economic or monetary chaos.*

A Simple Illustration of How
Gold Acts as an Inflation Hedge

To demonstrate gold's role as a hedge against inflation, let's create an extremely simplified economic model. We'll see later how true to life this model actually turns out to be.

Let's say that in our imagined economy, there exist 1,000 $1 bills and 10 ounces of gold. Both bills and gold are acceptable as "money"—as payment for goods and services. And, in this economy, goods and services consist of ten widgets. Widgets are all you can buy with your money, and to buy one widget, you have to pay one ounce of gold or $100 in paper money. In terms of what it will buy, therefore, each ounce of gold is worth $100.

Now, let's say the productivity of the economy has remained stable: There are still only ten widgets around. The amount of gold has also remained stable: There are still only 10 ounces around. But the government—for reasons ranging from the most noble to the most base—has more obligations than it has "income" in the form of taxes. It dare not raise taxes any higher, so it turns on the printing press, and out come 1,000 more $1 bills. The government pays off its extra obligations with these new bills. This is *monetary inflation.*

On the one hand, you can see that *price inflation* is going to be one result. There is no increase in goods and services (widgets), but there are a lot more $1 bills around in people's pockets. If you owned one of the relatively scarce widgets, to whom would you sell it? To the person who was willing to bid the highest price, of course. And if you wanted to buy a widget, you can bet it would cost you more than $100 to get one now.

On the other hand, we can also see a dramatic change in the relationship of gold to paper money. Remember, the supply of gold and the supply of goods and services (widgets) have remained constant, but the supply of paper money has doubled.

The *value of the gold,* in terms of the goods and services (widgets) it will buy, has remained constant. One ounce of gold will still buy you one widget. The *true value of the paper dollars,* on the other hand, has been slashed. If your savings consisted of 100 $1 bills, they would have bought you one widget before the inflation. Now they'll get you maybe one half of a widget. Your purchasing power has been cut roughly in half.

As for the *dollar price* of the gold, it has doubled with the inflation—from $100 to $200 an ounce. Before, there were 100 $1 bills in circulation for each ounce of gold; now there are twice as many. Before, $100 in paper money would buy the same amount (one widget) as one ounce of gold; now it takes $200 of the inflated paper money to buy the same amount.

In real life, of course, the mathematics are not that simple or precise. *But the process of what happens is amazingly similar to what we have just described in this model.* In real life, there is likely to be some increase in goods and services and some increase in the amount of gold, but there are often dramatic increases in the amount of paper money put into circulation by governments. What happens is exactly as we have described it here and in Chapter 10. The purchasing power of the paper money is slashed, the purchasing power of the gold remains constant or actually improves, and the "price" of gold in terms of paper dollars rises dramatically.

This is true both over the course of centuries and over turbulent shorter periods of time, such as the past two decades.

Gold as an Inflation Hedge

The most detailed and scholarly study of the value of gold has been done by University of California Professor Roy Jastram. In his book, *The Golden Constant* (Wiley, 1977), he proved that gold's purchasing power has remained remarkably constant "for centuries at a time. Indeed, its purchasing power in the middle of the twentieth century was very nearly the same as in the midst of the seventeenth century."

"The amazing aspect of this conclusion," says Professor Jastram, "is that this is not because gold eventually moves toward commodity prices, but because commodity prices return to gold."

We don't have to become history buffs to learn about the value of gold, though. We have just lived through a period of rampant inflation—the go-go decades of the 1960s and the '70s. Several studies show how gold performed during this period compared with other assets.

One of these studies, conducted by the International Gold Corporation, is summarized in Table 4, which compares assets for several periods, all ending December 31, 1981. That was the last year of rampant inflation in the major industrialized nations, so this table shows how well each asset performed as an inflation hedge.

The result? Gold outperformed all other categories of investments denominated in six major currencies. In all cases, gold also outperformed the Consumer Price Index (price inflation) by a very wide margin, and in most cases by a multiple of the CPI. Even in Switzerland, where the local currency is traditionally strong, gold was the best type of investment.

TABLE 4
Gold as an Asset
versus
Stocks, Bonds, Money Markets,
and the Rate of Inflation
in Six Major Countries

	PERIOD AVERAGES:		
	5 YEARS	10 YEARS	TOTAL PERIOD*
United States			
Gold	36.91	28.48	24.72
Stocks	11.04	7.52	6.08
Bonds	− 1.54		3.39
Money markets	9.91		7.90
Consumer prices**	10.48	8.70	7.52
Canada			
Gold	41.13	31.23	25.89
Stocks	23.19	12.22	10.88
Bonds	2.36		4.62
Money markets	11.69		9.82
Consumer prices**	10.09	9.25	7.80

Source: International Gold Corporation, Inc.
Total return = percent per annum, compounded for periods ending December 31, 1981

*For gold, stocks, and consumer prices, total period is 1968–1981. For bonds and money markets, owing to limitations of available data, total period is 1973–1981.

**Consumer prices = rate of increase.

	PERIOD AVERAGES:		
			TOTAL
	5 YEARS	10 YEARS	PERIOD*
England			
Gold	30.35	29.94	26.13
Stocks	19.45	15.09	11.71
Bonds	8.94		10.57
Money markets	13.13		12.91
Consumer prices**	13.19	14.75	12.75
Germany			
Gold	33.68	21.50	17.50
Stocks	3.74	5.99	4.60
Bonds	3.98		8.02
Money markets	6.86		5.99
Consumer prices**	4.50	4.92	4.86
Switzerland			
Gold	29.26	17.23	14.92
Stocks	2.39	2.42	3.05
Bonds	3.03		6.55
Money markets	3.80		3.91
Consumer prices**	3.68	4.33	4.82
Japan			
Gold	32.55	23.82	19.89
Stocks	12.75	11.83	15.18
Bonds	7.03		8.92
Money markets	6.38		5.39
Consumer prices**	5.38	9.13	8.81

But you don't have to accept the word of a gold partisan. Salomon Brothers is a prestigious Wall Street investment firm. It certainly is not considered part of the "gold bug" camp, yet its independent studies also reveal the superior performance of gold and other "hard" assets in periods of inflation.

Each year, Salomon Brothers compares the returns provided by fourteen different investments: stocks, bonds, Treasury bills, foreign exchange, housing, farmland, oil, silver, gold, U.S. coins, U.S. stamps, diamonds, Chinese ceramics, and fine art by old masters. They also measure these investments against the Consumer Price Index (CPI), making it easy to determine their *real* rates of return.

In all inflationary periods, gold has outpaced the rate of inflation, providing a healthy real rate of return.

Measured from June 1970 to June 1980, for example, the CPI increased 7.7 percent per annum. During this period, gold provided a compounded annual rate of return of 31.6 percent. It was second among the fourteen investments, outperformed only by oil.

You'd still be ahead if you bought gold in 1970 and held on to it through 1985—with the last five years dominated by disinflation. During this fifteen-year period, the CPI increased 7.1 percent per annum. Gold provided a compounded annual rate of return of 15.5 percent and was still third among the fourteen investments, outperformed only by oil and U.S. coins.

Gold Mutual Funds

The same type of performance record is evident when you compare mutual funds. Gold funds consistently rank at the top of the class when you compare long-term performance (five years or more) over a period of high inflation. You'll find these comparisons and rankings periodically in financial journals such as *Forbes, Barron's,* and *Money* magazine.

Barron's, for example, publishes the comparisons of Lipper Analytical Service four times a year. In inflationary periods, its "Performance Gauge" consistently shows gold funds occupying most of the top slots for mutual fund performance.

Similarly, *Money* magazine published its rankings of "Best-Performing Mutual Funds" in its March 1984 issue. Over the previous year—a period of relatively low inflation and a Wall Street bull market—*no* gold funds placed among the top twenty. But looking at the previous five years, which included years of double-digit inflation, gold funds occupied four of the five top slots.

When to Buy Gold: Getting Down
to Specifics

The general answer to the question, "When to buy gold?" is
obvious. You want to buy and hold gold in periods of antici-
pated inflation and increasing inflation. You want to unload
most of your gold when inflation starts to slow down.

But what about more specific timing? If you first bought gold
at the very beginning of 1980 and held on to it, you're probably
not very favorably disposed to the metal. You bought at the
crest of a feverish inflation-fed panic into gold, when its price hit
$850 an ounce. Then the price plunged to just under $300, and
six years later (after far less extreme movements) finally rose
above $400.

That, obviously, is not the way to buy gold as an inflation
hedge. Gold is not a magic wand. As with any other investment,
you want to buy low and sell high, and that requires some way
to establish a rational value guide to the price of gold, and some
way to determine where you stand in the inflation cycle. Precisely because it is so easy to fall in love with gold, you need an
analytical approach to buying and selling gold that will protect
you from the emotions and mob hysteria of the gold market.
That will be our next concern.

First, let's look at what the absolute floor price for gold
might be under a worst-case scenario.

Second, we will look at gold's role as an international monetary asset, and use that role to calculate a more realistic floor
price for gold.

And *third,* I will show you how to weigh the downside risk
against gold's upward price potential, then compare gold with a
theoretically risk-free investment to answer the question: Is this
a good time to buy gold?

A Worst-Case Price for Gold

What might be the absolute floor price for gold under a worst-
case scenario? One way to determine this, for any commodity, is
to look at what it costs to produce that commodity. If prices fall
below that level for any extended period of time, new supplies
to the market will soon dry up.

More than 80 percent of the gold mined in the West comes from South Africa. On the average, it costs $250 per ounce to get gold profitably out of the ground in South Africa.

The major U.S. producer, Homestake Mining Co., brings gold in at a profit at approximately $300 per ounce. Placer operations in the United States can also produce gold profitably at about $300 per ounce, give or take $50 per ounce depending upon the location. In a few instances (not enough to affect the supply of gold significantly), low-grade heap leaching can still be profitable at around $200 per ounce.

On balance, then, the floor price for gold—viewing it strictly as a commodity—would seem to be around $250 per ounce. Below that, there would be few new supplies at all.

Using another method, I arrive with a figure in the same ballpark. I have plotted U.S. wholesale prices from 1860 to the present and derived a compound growth rate. Applying that same compound growth rate to gold from 1860 to the present, I get a current price for gold—again viewing it strictly as a commodity—of approximately $235 per ounce. This is right in line with the break-even price for mining South African gold profitably.

For the reasons we are about to give, however, it is doubtful that gold prices will ever again be seen anywhere in the neighborhood of $235 or $250.

Calculating a Price for Gold
as an International Monetary Asset

The cost of producing a commodity is its rock-bottom price, but gold is not just another commodity. Gold is also an international monetary asset. A check of International Monetary Fund data shows that virtually every central bank in the world holds gold as a monetary reserve asset.

While gold and silver are often considered together as precious metals assets, it is important to note a critical difference between them at this point. Silver is *not* a monetary asset. No silver holdings are listed by any central bank. And when it comes down to the bottom line, gold will always be their choice. Its physical properties make gold more desirable. The fact that thirty-five to fifty times the dollar value can be transported for the same weight makes gold the clear preference for individuals and institutions physically moving metal around the world.

Now, how can we use gold's role as a monetary asset to calculate a value price for it? By comparing the size of the gold holdings of the world's central banks with their foreign exchange holdings. This gives us an implied value for gold at any time, including the present.

I have taken the total world foreign exchange holdings of all central banks from 1950 through the present, and put them into dollar terms. Over this period, the size of these exchange holdings has exploded dramatically. The amount of the banks' gold reserves has stayed relatively stable. This implies a rising value for gold over those years, which was indeed the experience of the marketplace.

In 1950, for example, the foreign exchange holdings were just a little over $17 billion. The central banks also held 949 million ounces of gold. By dividing 949 million into 17 billion, I get an implied value for gold at that time of $18.22 per ounce.

By 1965, the implied monetary value of gold had risen to $26.28. And by 1970, to $55.82 per ounce. Five years later we had a really big jump in foreign exchange holdings—they nearly tripled, while gold reserves remained fairly constant. That boosted the implied value of gold to $175.

Where do we stand today? Using the same methods, we arrive at a current monetary value price for gold of $345 per ounce.

Since gold *is* a monetary asset, this $345 figure is a more realistic floor price for gold than our previous figure of $235 to $250. And with gold trading in the $400 range as this book is being written, there is not much downside price risk.

Gold's Upward Price Potential

Gold's upward price potential depends on the prospects for inflation. Another round of inflation, such as we had in the late 1970s, will bring another increase in the central banks' foreign exchange holdings. Since their gold reserves can be expected to remain about the same, that would result in another sizable jump in the implied value of gold.

If we have another round of serious inflation, I have no

doubt that this increase in gold's implied monetary value will be exceeded by gold's actual price rise in the marketplace.

First of all, there is the American market for gold. When the last round of inflation began, few Americans were aware of gold's ability to hold its value in times of inflation. Indeed, relatively few Americans realized just how much inflation was cutting into the value of most of their traditional investments. That is *not* the situation today. Americans have been educated the hard way about inflation. At the first sign of renewed inflationary vigor, the movement to gold will begin.

Then there is the world market. In Japan, for example, the gold futures market is only a few years old. Not much activity took place in 1982 and 1983. Trading averaged about three hundred kilos per day. Things began changing rapidly in 1984, and volume rose to about one metric ton per day. By 1985 Japan was having a veritable gold rush. All of this was taking place, mind you, at a time when inflation was a "dead issue" in the major industrialized nations.

What, then, are the prospects for another round of high inflation? In Chapter 1, I explained why I think another inflationary bout is all but inevitable. And in Chapter 10, I will show you how to fine-tune the prognosis for inflation by identifying the three stages of the inflationary cycle.

Under most circumstances, you will want about 10 percent of your total portfolio invested in gold assets. The exact amount depends on the returns you are getting from the Treasury securities in your portfolio, as I will explain in Chapter 5 ("The Right Mix for Your Financial Coat of Armor"), as well as where we stand in the inflationary cycle.

How Much Gold Should You Buy?

Once Stage 1 of the inflationary cycle falls into place (see Chapter 10), I turn bullish on gold. At this point, you should start adding to the gold portion of your portfolio on a systematic basis. You won't have another opportunity to get gold at these bargain-basement prices.

Once Stage 2 falls into place, you should increase your gold holdings to half of whatever your eventual maximum position would be.

Once Stage 3 of the inflationary cycle falls into place, you want to move to your maximum position in gold.

To some institutions or individuals, a maximum position in gold might represent a large portion of their total investment pool. To others, the maximum position might be proportionately quite small. In Chapter 14, I suggest different portfolio mixes for investors in widely varying circumstances. As I've already noted, you will want about 10 percent of your total portfolio invested in gold assets under most circumstances. Gold should never be less than 5 percent of your total portfolio, and during periods of peak inflation it may constitute as much as 30 percent of your portfolio.

If you monitor the three-stage inflation cycle carefully, and follow my suggestions to come on *how* and *where* to buy gold, you should be in an excellent position to reap maximum profits.

The Single Best Method for Buying
Gold Profitably

Over the long run, the single best way to buy gold is through dollar cost averaging. There's nothing complex about this method. You simply determine how much you are going to invest in gold, and then do it on a systematic basis, making level or equal dollar commitments at regular preset times during the year.

Your personal and business needs will dictate whether your purchases will be made daily, weekly, monthly, or perhaps quarterly. In any case, you should design the plan at the outset and then stick to it. Do not let emotions change your plan. At just the point in the cycle when gold sentiment is the most negative, you will not tend to think positively about investing more money in it. It is exactly at this point, however, that you must discipline yourself to stick with your long-range plan.

Dollar cost averaging, you see, makes you a financial genius, because over any long period of time you have bought the fewest units of gold at its highest price and the most units of gold at its lowest price. How can you beat that?

It is vital to note that dollar cost averaging works to your advantage only when the price of the asset being purchased rises over the long term. Dollar cost averaging is an exceedingly dangerous program when used to accumulate an asset that declines in price over the long term. Since the price of gold can be expected to rise over the long term, dollar cost averaging is the ideal way to buy it.

It is also important always to keep gold's value guides in mind when deciding how much to invest in this way. When gold's price is above its value guides, you want to minimize your periodic commitments. Conversely, you want to commit more to this program when gold's price is near or below its value guides.

More Tips on How and Where to Buy Gold

The early 1980s were marked by the bankruptcies of major gold and silver promotional outfits, such as International Gold Bullion Exchange and Bullion Reserve of North America. The losses to individuals due to the failure of these two firms alone may have totaled $100 million. The newspapers were filled with pathetic stories of elderly couples who had lost their life savings, or a church congregation that had deposited its entire building fund with one of these hucksters, only to see it disappear down the drain.

Why did so many investors lose their shirts by dealing with firms like these?

First, they got a little too greedy. These firms, and others like them, were quite adept at offering deals that seemed too good to be true. As it turned out—and almost always does in situations such as these—their deals *were* too good to be true.

Second, these investors got caught up in "gold fever" and forgot that there's a downside as well as an upside to every market. Their emotions prevailed, and mob hysteria ensued. This happened to many firms, too, and when prices collapsed they got caught in a squeeze and took a tumble.

Third, these investors placed an incredible amount of trust in firms they had never heard of before, and in people about whom they knew absolutely nothing. Without investigating, they accepted the firms' claims to be storing their metal safely for them. They did not take possession of their gold, and when panic time came, there wasn't enough gold in the vault—and sometimes no gold at all. In one instance of supreme irony, the only "gold" in the firm's vault were some rectangular blocks of wood painted gold!

Invariably these firms had expensive, slick, four-color literature with imposing views of their "corporate headquarters," which sometimes turned out to be office buildings in which they merely rented space. But people fell for it. "If they're doing that well," they figured, "they must know what they're doing, and I'm going to get my share."

There is absolutely no reason for this to happen to you. If you have been burned in the past, learn from your experience and don't repeat the same mistakes. There are plenty of reliable firms to deal with, and plenty of safe ways in which to purchase your gold (or silver).

First, deal only with firms that are established, have a solid track record of doing business in a conservative way, and can furnish reliable bank and credit references. Be wary of new firms that pop up in a bull market. Some of these will be totally legitimate operations, but if you deal with them be especially careful by insisting on the following precautions.

Second, the safest way to hold physical gold (coins and bars) is by taking possession. If you're holding it in your hands, you know it exists, and if you have any doubts you can verify its authenticity by having it assayed.

Also, with large orders, you can insist on a sight draft. These allow you to inspect your gold before completing the transaction, with your local banker as intermediary. The bank takes your funds, and the dealer ships the gold to an officer of the bank. Once the coins or bars arrive, you inspect them and give your approval to the officer. At that point, the bank forwards your funds to the dealer and releases the coins to you. Moreover, you have the right to refuse the shipment if you have any questions about its authenticity.

Dealers don't actively promote the idea of sight drafts, since it slows their cash flow and involves considerable extra paperwork. Also, you may have to educate your local banker about the procedures involved. But it is your money that is at risk, and the extra effort is far safer than simply putting your check in the mail.

Third, if you buy a gold certificate rather than take possession of the physical metal, make certain the gold is insured by a reliable firm and that your pieces are stored and registered in *your* name, not the dealer's name.

Now let me tell you about some of the places where I like to do business.

Rhode Island Hospital Trust National Bank

Few investors know about the excellent gold services available from Rhode Island Hospital Trust National Bank. Perhaps it's the cryptic name, usually abbreviated to "Hospital Trust." And before you suggest that I'm biased toward my home state of Rhode Island, to which I plead guilty, let me say that I dealt with Hospital Trust long before my family and I moved to Newport.

Hospital Trust is an old-line, very conservative New England bank. It's a major-league outfit in every respect, and is now a subsidiary of RIHT Financial Services Corp., a $2 billion Providence financial services institution. Now for the surprise: Hospital Trust is also the largest supplier of industrial gold in the United States, with 42 percent of that market.

"How can this be," you may be asking, "since I've never heard of Hospital Trust?" The bank got its start in the gold market when the federal government stopped supplying gold to industry and granted Hospital Trust the first license to supply the metal to jewelry manufacturers in Rhode Island. This was before the free market in gold, of course, and Rhode Island happens to be a major jewelry center in the United States. Some years ago, Hospital Trust also entered the retail gold market to service individual investors. Both coins and certificates are available. Its commissions are competitive.

If you are interested in coins or bullion, Hospital Trust will be glad to deal with you and your bank via sight draft. To arrange the transaction, your banker can call Richard A. Pierson, vice president, at (800) 942-2409.

Hospital Trust has physical gold available for delivery in these sizes and forms:

Gold Coins

Chinese Panda coins
1⁄10 ounce coins

¼ ounce coins
½ ounce coins
1 ounce coins
Canadian Maple Leafs
⅒ ounce coins
¼ ounce coins
1 ounce coins
U.S. gold coins
½ ounce coins
1 ounce coins

Gold Bullion

Credit Suisse bars (with assay certificate)
1 gram
5 grams
¼ ounce
½ ounce
1 ounce
5 ounces
10 ounces

When you are dealing with a reputable firm like Hospital Trust, certificates make a lot of sense. The bank stores your gold for you, issuing you an individually numbered and registered certificate (receipt). You have no storage worries, and—unlike investments in coins or bullion—you never pay a fabrication or shipping fee, an assay charge, or sales tax. Your investment is extremely liquid, since you can buy or sell at any of Hospital Trust's offices, by mail, or by telephone.

At Hospital Trust, the minimum purchase amount for certificates is one ounce of gold. You receive a sales voucher and certificate immediately at the time of purchase, and the bank stores your gold either in its own vault or at an off-premises location. Either way, your metal in storage is insured against fire and theft by Lloyd's of London.

For more information: Rhode Island Hospital Trust National Bank, One Hospital Trust Plaza, Providence, RI 02903-2449, telephones (800) 942-2409 and (401) 278-8496.

Benham Certified Metals

Benham Certified Metals is part of the Benham Capital Manage-
ment Group (BCMG), which includes the Capital Preservation
Fund recommended in Chapter 2 ("U.S. Treasury Securities").
BCMG manages more than $2 billion for over 150,000 investors.

It is important to note that the Benham Certified Metals program does not involve any leverage programs or delayed delivery. They keep no inventory, and their employees work strictly
on salary (not commission). They cannot offer investment advice, although they will try to supply information you need to
make your own decisions. These are all *advantages*. You are not
involved in the more speculative forms of precious metals investments.

Benham Certified Metals (BCM) can offer you Canadian
Maple Leafs and gold bars in a variety of sizes and weights.
BCM will also attempt to obtain other metals for an individual
investor with a specific interest.

When you buy precious metals from BCM, you pay the
wholesale price plus 1 percent commission. BCM will buy back
metals you bought from it, for 1 percent below wholesale.
Benham's wholesale price typically runs 2 to 4 percent over spot
(the price the big dealers have to pay), depending on market
conditions. The minimum transaction amount is $2,000 for gold.

When you deal with BCM, several storage options are available. You can have the metal shipped to you or to the depository of your choice. Benham can store your investment in
their bank depository trust account at the Bank of Delaware, or
they can help you establish your own storage account there. Finally, they can arrange for storage of your metals in Switzerland.

The Bank of Delaware has been in business for almost two
centuries. It has over $1 billion in assets, and every major bank,
brokerage firm, and dealer actively engaged in precious metals
maintains a relationship with this bank. Its storage accounts are
held at the Bank of Delaware Depository, 519 North Market
Street, Wilmington, DE 19899.

Benham gives you the types of protection every investor
should insist upon before selecting a dealer. All the metals they
store for customers are *segregated*. This means that your gold or
silver is registered as your property, distinct from the assets of

either the Bank of Delaware or Benham Certified Metals. This protects your metals from any possible creditor claims against either company, or bankruptcy on the part of either company.

The Benham group has also taken additional precautions to safeguard your investment. First, you get a confirmation mailed on the day of the transaction. Second, you receive a depository receipt from the Bank of Delaware, listing the commodity type and quantity stored on your behalf. Third, BCM includes a complete inventory of all of your metals on deposit with each semi-annual billing for storage fees. And fourth, twice a year the nationally recognized accounting firm of Peat, Marwick, Mitchell & Co. performs on-site inventories of BCM's holdings at the Bank of Delaware.

For more information: Benham Certified Metals, 755 Page Mill Road, Palo Alto, CA 94304, telephone (800) 447-GOLD.

ASA Limited

ASA is a one-of-a-kind investment vehicle. Because it is a South African corporation, however, you may not want to include it in your portfolio. I leave that judgment to you and merely wish to call your attention to its unique characteristics.

ASA, you see, is a closed-end gold fund* traded on the New York Stock Exchange. As an investment, ASA has been in the past—and will be in the future—an excellent proxy for gold. As a security listed on the big board, ASA is easier to trade than any open-end gold fund. It also makes more financial sense than trading the penny stocks or most of the North American mines, which simply are not in a comparable league to the South African mines in ASA's portfolio.

From an investment standpoint, ASA is excellent inflation insurance. Down the line, ASA's price will rise to reflect long-term inflationary problems. Its volatility and reasonable volume also make ASA an excellent stock for traders. (ASA's price fluctuates substantially more than bullion prices.)

ASA Limited is incorporated in the Republic of South Africa and has its offices in Johannesburg. By charter, more than 50

---

*Most mutual funds are "open-ended"—they issue as many shares as there are buyers, at a set price per share. A "closed-end" mutual fund is like a corporate stock: Only a stipulated number of shares is available, and the price rises or falls depending on investor demand.

percent of its assets must be in common shares of South African mining companies. A substantial portion of the remainder must be in other South African companies. At the end of February 1985, ASA's assets totaled $414 million.

Unlike most closed-end investment funds, ASA's portfolio is not widely diversified. In fact, the majority of the fund's two dozen holdings are in only five mines. These are Driefontein Consolidated (a combination of the old East and West Driefonteins), Kloof, Southvaal, Vaal Reefs, and Winklehaak.

ASA's portfolio turnover can only be described as nonexistent. In 1982, 1983, and 1984, portfolio turnover was less than 1 percent per year. It is normal for most institutional portfolios to turn over between 30 percent and 100 percent per year.

You can follow ASA's price in the New York Stock Exchange listings in your newspaper. As a NYSE-listed security, its price reflects supply and demand, not asset value as in the case of open-end funds. Over time ASA will sell at a premium or discount to its underlying asset value.

Manfra, Tordella and Brookes, Inc.

Manfra, Tordella and Brookes (MTB) is America's largest independent wholesaler of precious metals and foreign bank notes. MTB trades about 10 percent of the annual worldwide production of Canadian Maple Leafs, South African Krugerrands, and Mexican gold coins. Its computer-updated prices are made available to the industry via Reuters and Tele-rate, and it is generally accepted that MTB's coin quotation system is the most complete available in the world today.

Around a thousand banks nationwide offer their customers retail precious metals services through MTB. You should ask for MTB's booklet on investing and collecting gold coins. You will find information on a number of my favorite coins, such as the Swiss 20 franc, the Austrian 4 ducat, and the Mexican 50 peso.

For information: Manfra, Tordella and Brookes, Inc., 30 Rockefeller Plaza, New York, NY 10012, telephone (800) 223-5818 or (212) 621-9500. Also at One Biscayne Tower, Miami, FL 33131, telephone (305) 374-1007. If you can start with an investment of a few thousand dollars, I advise calling MTB's retail or personal investor department at (800) 535-7481 or (212) 621-9502. If you are an institutional investor, call (800) 223-5818 or (212) 621-9500.

Tips for the Novice Gold Coin Collector

If you are buying and selling gold coins strictly as a precious metals investment, it is probably best to stick with coins that are universally recognized and thus extremely liquid. U.S. Saint-Gaudens and Liberty coins come immediately to mind.

If you are planning to collect gold coins on a systematic basis and particularly admire their beauty, you may want to include some U.S gold and silver commemoratives and Mexican gold coins in your portfolio.

And if you are interested in collecting gold coins that sell at a premium because of their rarity, I would advise you to start with U.S. coins. Specific suggestions on Mexican and U.S. coins follow.

Numismatic Gradings and Dealers

I have two problems with numismatics: grading and dealers. I believe that many coins are graded, shall we say, aggressively. (See Table 5 for an explanation of numismatic coin gradings.)

I find it difficult to distinguish an MS (mint state) 60 from, say, an MS 61 or 62. These distinctions are often subjective guesses. As for the top grade, MS 65s are difficult to accumulate and are not without considerable grading controversy even among experts.

I like MS 65s only for the most sophisticated and specialized collector. An MS 65 is an esoteric coin that will show enormous relative potential in a big gold market. In a flat or down market, however, you may have problems selling your MS 65 coins for what you might reasonably expect.

As for the dealers, too many are promotional hucksters. There are hundreds of dealers in the United States and most are "mom and pop" type operations. Many have been in business for years and have developed local reputations for integrity and fair dealing. I am not referring to them. Nor am I referring to the reputable, prime dealers, such as Manfra, Tordella and Brookes. The hucksters to avoid are those promoting commemoratives, silver oddities, arcane foreign objects, and low-graded U.S. coins. I would also advise you to stay away from private mint offerings. They are heavily promoted and grossly over-priced.

Instead, concentrate on quality, widely recognized, and (for my money) rare U.S. coins.

Rare U.S. Gold Coins

Why do I recommend rare U.S. gold coins above others? First, I believe the average investor/collector will become a *better* investor/collector by specializing in one sector of the gold coin market. Second, this can make investing enjoyable, as you become more expert at what you're doing, which always increases the fun. Third, the community of interest and availability of information is greater for U.S. coins than for most other gold coin series.

Your interest should center on gold dollars, quarter eagles ($2.50 Liberty and Indian Head types), half eagles ($5 Indian Head and Liberty types), eagles ($10 Indian and Eagle coins), and double eagles ($20 Saint-Gaudens and Liberty coins). Three-dollar gold is extremely rare and appropriate only for the most ardent collector.

As a rule of thumb, the smaller the coin, the more difficult it will be to acquire it in quantity. A $20 double eagle will be easier to buy than a $1 Liberty, Indian Princess, or Indian Head. In $10 eagles, the Liberty is easier to accumulate than the Indian. And Saint-Gaudens coins are generally preferable over Liberty double eagles.

In summary, I advise the beginning collector to concentrate on rare U.S. coins in the MS 60 and 63 grades. If you are just starting out, your most logical choice probably would be a few MS 60 Saint-Gaudens-type double eagles. These give you, in effect, a double play on gold. For example, the one-ounce Canadian Maple Leaf was recently quoted at $359, while an MS 60 common date $20 Saint-Gaudens (minted between 1907 and 1933) was quoted at $575. The Maple Leaf will never be worth more than bullion prices, plus a small premium. The $20 Saint-Gaudens has enormous collector appeal and gives you an opportunity to benefit both from a general long-term price increase in gold and from a potentially sizable numismatic price increase.

The next step is to move up to higher-grade mint state U.S. rare gold pieces, including the beautiful and historically significant eleven U.S. commemoratives minted between 1903 and 1926. The private and territorial U.S. gold coins minted in the 1800s are also of great interest to sophisticated and substantial investors.

Mexican Gold Coins

For beauty, I find the gold coins of Mexico to be of particular interest. These coins have been the best-selling series in the world, exceeding the sales of South African and Canadian coins combined. Mexico's one-ounce, half-ounce, and quarter-ounce coins also give investors the opportunity to purchase Mexican gold coins at even weights, so you can easily determine how much you are paying per ounce of gold. These even-weight coins are legal tender in Mexico. Banco de Mexico (the Central Bank of Mexico) guarantees full redemption at a price based upon the current market value of gold.

A particularly interesting coin, beautiful in jewelry, is Mexico's 50 peso Centenario. At 1.2057 troy ounces of pure gold, it is the heavyweight of gold bullion coins. More than 17 million of these have been sold worldwide. Originally minted in 1921, it was restruck in 1947 and continues to be minted in unlimited quantities.

Other choices in the Mexican gold coins series are the 2 peso, the 2½ peso Hidalgo, the 5 peso Hidalgo, the 10 peso Hidalgo, and the 25 peso Azteca. All are beautiful coins.

My gold company, Newport Rare Gold, Inc., offers rare gold coins for investment. Call (800) 843-RARE for a free information packet. Of all my regular research projects, none is as exciting as these rare coins.

TABLE 5
Numismatic Coin Gradings

The following are the general characteristics that define the different coin gradings. (Listed from lowest grade to highest.)

Poor or Fair (Mint state 1 to 3): Designs and lettering partially visible, quite worn.

G or Good (Mint state 4 to 6): Legends, design and date are clear.

F or Fine (Mint state 12 to 15): All major details will be visible but will show definite wear.

VF or Very Fine (Mint state 20 to 30): More details will be visible with the major details virtually complete.

EF, XF or Extra Fine (Mint state 40 to 45): Light wear on the high points with some mint lustre present.

AU or About Uncirculated (Mint state 50 to 55): Small trace of wear visible on the highest points with at least half of the mint lustre still present.

UNC or Uncirculated (Mint state 60 to 65): No trace of wear, with some small nicks or marks present.

PF or Proof: Coins specially struck for collectors. Usually mirror-like surface. Sand blast and matte proof in some series.

When grading coins any defects should be noted, such as bent, scratched, etc. Cleaning or mutilations of any kind should be mentioned (i.e., Extra Fine with rim nick at 9 o'clock, small scratch on face).

Source: Manfra, Tordella and Brookes, Inc.

TABLE 6
Gold Measurements and Characteristics

The Weight of Gold

1 oz t	= 31.1033 gms	24 grains	= 1 dwt
1 oz t	= 480 grs	5.760 grains	= 1 lb t
1 oz t	= 20 dwt	15,432 grains	= 1 kg
12 oz t	= 1 lb t	437.5 grains	= 1 oz av
14.5833 oz t	= 1 lb av	7,000 grains	= 1 lb av
0.9114 oz t	= 1 oz av	1 grain	= 0.0648 gm
32.15 oz t	= 1 kg	240 dwt	= 1 lb t
1 gram	= 5.3 kts (Roman)	643.01 dwt	= 1 kg
1 gram	= 15.432 grs	18.2291 dwt	= 1 oz av
1 gram	= 0.643 dwt	291.666 dwt	= 1 lb av
1.5552 grams	= 1 dwt	1 kg	= 2.68 lbs t
1,000 grams	= 1 kg	1 kg	= 35.2740 ozs av
28.3495 grams	= 1 oz av	1 kg	= 2.2046 lbs av

Metric System Versus Troy System

1 metric ton	= 1,000 kg	1 troy pound	= 12 ozs t
1 kilogram	= 1,000 grams	1 troy ounce	= 10 dwt
1 gram	= 1,000 mgs	1 dwt	= 24 grains

The troy system is due to be replaced in the United States with the metric system in the 1980s. The metric system is currently in use in all of Europe, Latin America and most other countries of the world.

Fineness (Fine Gold Content)

Actual gold content exclusive of the other metal(s) in the alloy. Usually expressed in grams or troy oz. Pure gold is 24 karats. The fineness is expressed in thousandths parts of an alloy. Pure gold is 1.000 or 24 karats. .750 (seven hundred and fifty parts of gold contained in 1000 parts of alloy) is known as 18 karats. The relationship of fineness to karats is all proportional. All of the American and Mexican along with some of the Austrian gold coins are .900 fine.

Fineness (or Purity of Gold Equivalency)

24 karats = 1000 fine		20 karats = 833.3 fine	
23 karats = 958.3 fine		18 karats = 750 fine	
22 karats = 916.6 fine		16 karats = 666.7 fine	
21.6 karats = 900.0 fine		14 karats = 583.3 fine	
21 karats = 875 fine		10 karats = 416.6 fine	

Measurements

1 inch	= 25.40 millimeters
1 millimeter	= .0394 inches

Face Value

The original monetary value of a coin. A $20 United States gold coin was worth exactly twenty dollars at the time it was minted by the U.S. Government. Face values no longer have an influence on gold coins, because in most cases they are no longer legal tender, and their value is measured in terms of rarity along with the current value of the actual precious metal contained in the coin.

Intrinsic Value

The actual current value of the metal used in the coin.

Premium

Market value of the coin less the intrinsic value of the same represents the premium. A gold coin which contains $100 in gold (intrinsic value) and sells for $120 (market value) has a 20 percent premium.

Counterfeit

Also known as **forgery**. A coin not manufactured by the original authority of issuance. Counterfeit coins are usually made of gold (but not necessarily of the same fineness) and are used to defraud collectors. Counterfeits are well made in most cases and cannot be distinguished by the average collector. The integrity and knowledge of the dealer is in this case of utmost importance to the collector when buying coins.

Restrike

Also known as **new minting**. Coins made by the government of the country of original issue. The original die is used to manufacture these coins. Restriking of gold coins has become a very profitable business for Austria and Mexico, as these countries have taken full advantage of the ever increasing worldwide demand for low premium gold coins.

Source: Manfra, Tordella and Brookes, Inc.

· FOUR ·

Silver

Silver is another plate in the Financial Armadillo's coat of armor because it performs so well in times of inflation. Indeed, my research has led me to believe that silver may be more undervalued today than gold, and that it could make extraordinary gains in a new round of serious price inflation.

I say this even though I have reservations about the usual argument put forth by silver bulls—that the "gap" between new mine production and industrial consumption will propel prices upward. The basic theory is correct over the long run, but some silver advocates misuse it to build an overly euphoric case for silver. At any rate, I have other compelling reasons to be bullish on silver in times of inflation.

Gold and silver are usually lumped together as "precious metals" investments. However, it is important to note the major difference between the two.

Silver is an industrial metal. It is, of course, a rare industrial metal, but it is not a monetary metal in any primary sense. Any monetary value for silver is simply an implied value, though a case might be made that silver has some monetary value in India.

Gold, on the other hand, is a monetary metal in the primary sense. It has industrial uses, but they are secondary to its monetary role. Gold is held as a reserve asset by the majority of the world's central banks, while silver is not held as a monetary asset by any of them. The International Monetary Fund's reserve records do not list a single ounce of silver.

This distinction has both positive and negative connotations for silver. Industrial sluggishness can work to depress the price of silver. On the other hand, the fact that no central bank holds silver as a monetary asset means that central banks cannot depress or control the price of silver by intervening in a free market.

Gold definitely should be included as a building block in

your Financial Armadillo Strategy. Silver may be added, but only as fine tuning.

Silver's Performance in Times
of Inflation

Salomon Brothers, the Wall Street investment firm, annually tracks the performance of fourteen different kinds of investments, including silver. The Salomon Brothers survey shows that silver did very well in the inflationary decade extending from June 1970 to June 1980. It placed fourth among the fourteen different types of investments, with a compounded annual rate of return of 23.7 percent, while the Consumer Price Index was rising 7.7 percent per annum. Only oil, gold, and U.S. coins performed better.

In the disinflationary 1980s, on the other hand, silver was the worst of the fourteen investments. From June 1980 to June 1985, its compounded annual rate of return was a *negative* 15.9 percent, even while price inflation was 5.7 percent per annum.

Financial author Howard J. Ruff got similar results when he commissioned a computer study of the performance of many different investments in varying economic climates. The results were presented in the April 1, 1985, issue of his *Financial Success Report.*

Ruff found that silver was the *most* profitable investment in the highly inflationary period from August 1976 to January 1980. Its price increased 984 percent, or 699 percent adjusted for inflation. It performed far better than even South African gold shares, gold, or platinum. On the other hand, silver was the *worst* investment in the disinflationary period from January 1980 to February 1985. It decreased in value by 87 percent, or 90.5 percent when adjusted for inflation. It fell harder than platinum, gold, or copper.

Looking at the entire period from August 1976 to February 1985, gold funds and South African gold stocks still did very well despite the disinflationary 1980s. They placed third and sixth on Ruff's list of the "Top Twenty Gainers" for this total period. But silver was nowhere on the Top Twenty list. The lesson, I think, is clear. Silver is an excellent investment in times of high inflation, but it falls very hard when the rate of inflation slows down. It is very important to time your silver investments with the inflationary cycle foremost in mind, and I will show you how to do that in this chapter.

The Gap Between New Mine Production
and Industrial Demand for Silver

The favorite argument of most silver bulls is that silver's price must rise over the long run because of the gap between industrial demand and new mine production. In short, there isn't enough mining activity to supply the industrial demand. The deficit is obtained from "secondary supplies"—U.S. Treasury sales of silver and the meltdown of old silver coins, silverware, jewelry from India, and so forth.

The tables that follow present an accurate portrait of the silver "gap," as it is known. If you are the sort who thrives on figures and charts, you can use these to check my reasoning. If you're not statistically minded, you can ignore them; indeed, if you wish, you can proceed to page 94. As we shall see, the gap supports a bullish case for silver over the long term, but it's not essential to a bullish position. Since the gap plays such a prominent role in silver literature and strategies, however, I do want to analyze it objectively and set the record straight.

As we shall see, a primary deficit *has* been recorded for over twenty years. The nature of this deficit, however, deserves some attention. The deficit is not quite what it appears to be on the surface.

Table 7 allows us to analyze consumption, mine production, and secondary supplies over a twenty-five-year period. The first thing to note is that there has been very little growth in industrial demand for silver over the past twenty-five years. In fact, industrial consumption for the year 1985—374 million ounces— is not significantly more than 1966's industrial consumption of 348 million ounces. That's an overall increase of just 7.5 percent in nineteen years. In comparison, the gross national product of the United States jumped from $658 billion in 1966 to $3,998 billion in 1985, an increase of 608 percent.

We also find that the heyday of the primary deficits—the gap between industrial consumption and mine production—was in the early 1960s, and that the increases in that deficit resulted in large measure from substantial increases in coinage. In 1961, coinage consumption totaled 137 million ounces. By 1965, this had grown to 381 million ounces.

Table 8 shows that, from 1961 through 1969, secondary supplies obtained from U.S. Treasury sales were more than enough to make up for the amount of silver used in coinage in the non-Communist world.

It is important to eliminate coinage when judging the overall consumption trends for silver over the past twenty-five years. In Table 9, therefore, coinage and U.S. Treasury sales have been removed from the overall review. Two important facts then become clear:

1. Mine production is not sufficient to meet industrial needs, even taking into account the very modest growth in that industrial demand over the past twenty-five years.

2. Mine production has grown over the past twenty-five years, and seems largely to ignore cycles of economic expansion and contraction. In fact, there was no growth in mine production between 1970 and 1980.

Why Have Mine Production and Industrial Demand Been So Sluggish?

Why hasn't silver mine production increased to close the gap between supply and demand? Indeed, why has industrial demand itself remained so sluggish?

Looking first at mine production, we find that there simply isn't enough silver readily available in the earth's crust. That is what makes silver a *rare* metal, after all. As for what could potentially be extracted, silver prices simply haven't been high enough over the long run to spur a major jump in mine production. As we shall see shortly, other sources of secondary supplies have been available, at prices lower than the cost of mining that much extra silver.

This is especially true since most mined silver is a byproduct of other minerals. In fact, on a worldwide basis, approximately 70 percent of all newly mined silver is a byproduct of copper, lead, and zinc mining. It is *their* prices, not silver's price, that usually determine whether the mines are profitable and whether mining activities shall be expanded. In the 1980s, certainly, the demand for copper, lead, and zinc has not been growing enough to produce significant increases in silver byproduct.

In the United States the situation is somewhat altered. Table 10 shows that in 1984 the seven largest U.S. silver-producing mines were primarily silver mines. The different composition of silver mining in the United States is not enough, however, to alter the basic dependence of silver on other metals worldwide.

Why, then, hasn't industrial demand for silver grown with the economy? The primary reason is that manufacturers have learned both how to reduce their need for silver and how to find cheaper substitutes. This has been a long-term trend, but it was spurred by the severe run-up of silver prices in the late 1970s. That price explosion convinced manufacturers that they needed to find substitutes for silver, and in large part, they have.

Table 11 shows the end-uses of silver processed by U.S. manufacturers. U.S. consumption constitutes 35 to 40 percent of total industrial consumption in the non-Communist world, and U.S. usage patterns are fairly representative of worldwide patterns.

The largest category of silver use has been in photography. As Table 11 shows, the amount of silver used in photography in the United States jumped from 49.5 million ounces in 1974 to 66 million ounces in 1979. Since then, however, there has been a decline in photographic use. Eastman Kodak and other manufacturers have learned how to reduce the amount of silver used in the photographic process, and they hope eventually to eliminate the need for silver.

Other areas of silver usage have actually contracted sharply. Manufacture of sterling silverware, for example, peaked at 29 million ounces in 1973 and has come down sharply since. We see the same pattern in some other categories, and there are no categories showing enough growth to make up for these losses.

Clearly, higher silver prices have decimated certain sectors of the silver market, and these sectors are unlikely to show much resilience in the future.

Secondary Supplies of Silver:
What Price Makes Them Available?

I mentioned earlier that secondary supplies of silver are available at lower cost than it would require to mine sufficient extra silver. For one thing, the U.S. Treasury sells some of its silver stockpile as needed to meet industrial demands, as it did between 1961 and 1970. What other secondary supplies meet the gap between industrial demand and new mine production?

Primarily, the gap, or "primary deficit," is met by the meltdown of old coins, bullion, silverware, and jewelry. (There is also some recycling of silver from used X-ray films.) This is a classic supply-and-demand situation. As the price for silver rises, more and more people sell their coins, bullion, silverware, or jewelry for the price it brings. When the price rises high enough—as it did in the late 1970s—silver smelters work around the clock. In recent years, though, it's been a pretty leisurely business.

Nobody knows for certain, of course, exactly how much silver is available from these secondary sources. The most exhaustive attempt to find out was a 144-page report entitled *The Price Responsiveness of Secondary Silver,* prepared in 1981–82 by Economic Consulting Services, Inc., of Washington, D.C., for the U.S. Bureau of Mines. This study was placed on open file on May 14, 1982. It concluded as follows:

> It has been determined that there are very large unreported stocks of silver bullion and coins in the U.S. which under certain conditions can become an important source of future incremental supply to the market. . . . The total volume of these unreported stocks is estimated to be 1.6 billion ounces at year end 1980. . . . Of these stocks, roughly 61 percent are held rather widely among the general population in the form of coins. . . . In addition to large silver stocks of bullion and coins, U.S. individuals hold approximately 850 million ounces of silver in the form of sterlingware which, under certain circumstances, can also contribute significantly to the market. That's a total of 2.45 billion ounces.

It appears, then, that investors and speculators hold a great deal of silver. Most of this, however, is being held as a long-term store of value, and won't become available until the price is right. And what might that price be? The Bureau of Mines study reported that "secondary refiners interviewed were unanimous that at *a real silver price of $15 to $20 an ounce,* secondary silver available in the marketplace would increase in absolute volume by quite a large magnitude" (emphasis added).

As I see it, these are the conclusions most relevant to holding silver as a long-term investment:

1. A real gap does exist between industrial demand for silver and new mine production.

2. Industrial demand is stable, not rising dramatically, as is sometimes portrayed in pro-silver literature.

3. Nevertheless, even with stable industrial demand, the gap or primary deficit cannot help but give a bullish tone to silver over the long run. Year after year, those secondary supplies are being depleted.

To illustrate this point, let us accept the highest figure in the Bureau of Mines study. We will assume that 2.45 billion ounces of silver, including the sterling silver in your dining room buffet, was available as secondary supplies at the end of 1980. Since 1980 the annual primary deficit has been approximately 60 million ounces. That means that by the end of 1995, nearly a billion ounces of these secondary supplies will have been consumed to meet the gap. At the same time, new mine supplies are also being depleted. Unless sizable and totally new supplies of silver are discovered—and for geological reasons that's not likely— Father Time will be bullish on silver.

All of this, mind you, is not even considering inflation as a factor or reason to invest in silver. It is looking at silver strictly as an industrial commodity.

Some Other Potential Factors in Silver Supply and Demand

Silver bulls sometimes paint various scenarios that would result in a quantum jump in demand for silver. At the same time, other hard-to-quantify factors enter the supply side of the equation. Let us look at these briefly.

War

During World War II, about 900 million ounces of silver were used by the United States and its allies. Without doubt, demand would increase substantially if significant military hostilities erupt in the future. On the other hand, there is the very real possibility that various governments would confiscate silver, or take action to set its price, due to military needs.

U.S.S.R.

The Soviet Union, long a substantial producer and user of silver, has begun to import silver in recent years. As you might imagine, reliable statistics and projections are impossible to obtain. There is little question that industrial demand in the Soviet Union will increase at least modestly, as it is doing in the United States and elsewhere in the industrialized world. However, there is no reason at this point to think such demand would skew world market price trends.

China

There is also some talk about a substantial increase in demand for silver in mainland China. Once again, hard statistics are not available. Over the past few years, I have made several trips to Hong Kong and have posed this question to a number of authorities in that area of the world. It is my view that modernization of China's economic infrastructure will develop only at a very slow pace over the next five years. Because such growth comes off a very low base, *incremental* increases in demand for any consumer or industrial product will be high. As a result, the Chinese influence on world silver markets cannot be anything but positive, although it is premature to assume a major impact in the near future.

India

A substantial hoard of silver exists in India. Once again, good statistics are not available. The U.S. Bureau of Mines assumes a figure of 5 billion ounces, but there is no way to validate that figure and it appears to be very much on the high side. Over the past five years, India has provided *ever-decreasing* levels of silver to the world's secondary markets. In 1978, 46 million ounces were supplied by India, and by 1985 only 26 million ounces.

In short, all of the above factors are unknown quantities. As such, I do not take them into consideration when determining whether to invest in silver. On balance, though, I think they do add a bullish tone to the prospects for silver over the long run.

A Worst-Case Price for Silver

What might be the absolute floor price for silver under a worst-case scenario? As we saw in our discussion of gold, one way to determine this scenario for any commodity is to look at what it costs to produce that commodity. If prices fall below that level for any extended period of time, new supplies to the market will soon dry up.

In the United States, Hecla Mining Company's Ranchers Exploration and Development mine in Utah is an extremely profitable mine and produces silver at a break-even point of about $4.50 to $5 per ounce. This is perhaps the lowest extraction cost for any sizable silver mine in the United States. Elsewhere in the world, it costs $15 and more to mine an ounce of silver. With current prices far below that level, you can see why silver production is so sluggish. The rest of the world's contribution to silver production is largely as a byproduct of the mining of other minerals that are used in far greater quantities by industry.

It would seem, then, that $4.50 per ounce is a basic floor price for silver, based on its cost of production. At today's market prices, there is not much down-side risk with silver.

Four Reasons Why I Think Silver
Is Undervalued

As with gold, I use various methods to arrive at a value target for silver's price. It is very important to remain as objective as possible when evaluating any investment, especially one such as silver or gold, about which it is so easy to become involved emotionally.

First, then, I look at wholesale price trends. In the United States, the original Coinage Act of April 2, 1792, set a mint ratio of 15 to 1 between gold and silver. The two metals were to trade at prices set by that ratio. At that time, the world gold price was $19.39 per ounce, so the actual price of silver was $1.29 per ounce.

I have calculated a compound growth rate for wholesale prices in the United States from that date (April 2, 1792) to the present. I have then applied the same compounding factor to the base price for silver of $1.29 in 1972. *Based on this trend in wholesale prices, I arrive at a current price for silver of $15.41 per ounce. This is the price that silver would sell at today if it were to match the compounded growth rate of all wholesale commodities since 1792.*

Next, I compare worldwide production of silver and gold. Over the past twenty years, silver has tended to be mined, in relationship to gold, at a ratio ranging from 6 to 1 to 9 to 1, with an upward trend. I think a silver-to-gold ratio of 9 to 1 is a legitimate current ratio, given worldwide production levels.

Next, I look at the availability of gold and silver within the earth's crust. A geological study of the various elements shows that silver is available in the earth's crust at an abundance approximately ten times that of gold. This relationship is very similar to the actual production relationship between silver and gold.

Next, I look at total available resources for gold and silver. A recent study by the U.S. Geological Service showed a ratio of approximately 12 to 1. Once again, this is pretty much in line with the other ratios.

The 15 to 1 ratio set by the Coinage Act of 1792 was quite arbitrary, and really of little significance in the current scheme of things. Over the past ten years, silver and gold have tended to trade at a ratio of 35 to 1. This ratio has dropped at times into the 20s and has moved at other times into the 70s, but on balance a ratio of 35 to 1 has applied in recent years. This ratio is analytically far too conservative, however. A ratio of 10 to 1 more reasonably outlines the true relationship of silver to gold as these elements currently are found worldwide.

As we saw in Chapter 3, my research assigns a current commodity value for gold of approximately $235 per ounce, and a monetary-based value for gold of about $345 per ounce. Since silver is not a monetary asset, however, it is perhaps more appropriate to look at the inflation-adjusted commodity price for gold of $235 per ounce. Using a 10-to-1 ratio of silver to gold, I derive an appropriate price for silver of approximately $23.50 per ounce. This is right in line with the estimate by the U.S. Bureau of Mines study that real prices of $15 to $20 would be necessary to bring a large increase in secondary supplies to the market.

As I write, silver is trading at about $5 per ounce. That places it far below my value target price of $23.50. At current market prices, silver can be considered an excellent purchase to hold for long-term appreciation.

How Much Silver Belongs in
Your Portfolio? A Three-Step Timing Strategy

As with gold, the silver in your portfolio should be acquired on a dollar cost averaging basis. To review this concept, see pages 71–73 of Chapter 3.

I recommend that your maximum position in any single type of investment be limited to 10 percent of your total portfolio. This is true whether we're talking about silver, Persian rugs, or avocado acreage. None of us is right all the time, so it makes sense to diversify. The 10 percent limit demonstrates proper respect for the unknown.

When I refer to your "maximum position," therefore, I am referring to 10 percent of your total portfolio.

Also, keep in mind silver's responsiveness to the inflationary cycle. As we saw at the beginning of this chapter, silver may be your best investment in times of surging inflation, but it can also be your worst-performing asset in noninflationary or disinflationary times. Our maximum holdings, therefore, are reserved for periods of inflationary surges, and the best time to acquire these holdings is just before that inflationary cycle begins, when silver prices are likely to be at their lowest point.

With 10 percent as your maximum position in silver, let us say that you are willing to commit yourself to 6 percent when "the price is right"—that is, before the inflationary surge begins. Once Stage 2 of the inflationary cycle falls into place (see Chapter 10), boost this to 8 percent. And when Stage 3 of the inflationary cycle falls into place, proceed to your maximum position of 10 percent.

Now for some fine tuning with that first 6 percent commitment to silver. Let's divide that into 2 percent increments, and time your commitments to three indicators. In other words, as each of these three indicators falls into place, you commit 2 percent of your total portfolio to silver. Meanwhile, if the inflationary cycle falls into place, you increase your holdings accordingly.

Our *first* indicator is the ratio of the silver price to the gold price. As we've seen, that ratio has ranged in recent years from 20 to 1 to as high as 70 to 1, with an average ratio of 35 to 1 prevailing. Let us set a framework, then, of 10 to 70 as a spread, with 35 to 1 as a norm. At a ratio above 35 to 1, silver is undervalued in relation to gold, taking into account its recent price history. Therefore, a ratio above 35 to 1 is your first indicator to start buying silver.

The *second* indicator is a nominal price for silver below $10 per ounce. By nominal price I mean a current market price unadjusted for inflation. At these low prices (below $10), very little scrap silver or secondary silver is entering the market, certainly not enough to allow refiners to build up inventory beyond the norm. Also, prices below $10 per ounce are comfortably below any of our value price targets mentioned earlier.

The *third* indicator is a negative real rate of return from Treasury bills. If that happens, you want to offset your loss of returns from that investment by increasing your holdings in silver.

Thus we have three indicators that are not tied to the inflationary cycle, and the three stages of the inflationary cycle itself. Using 2 percent building blocks or increments, we can use these indicators and stages to decide how much of our total portfolio should be in silver.

As I write, the first two indicators are in place—silver's price ratio to gold is very high, about 65 to 1, and the nominal market price is way below $10 per ounce. T-bills are providing a real, inflation-adjusted return, however, and the inflationary cycle has not fallen into place. I would limit my silver investments, therefore, to approximately 4 percent of my total portfolio.

Once Stage 1 of the inflationary cycle falls into place (see Chapter 10), I would increase my commitment to 6 percent, even if T-bills continue to provide a real rate of return. In fact, I'd commit 6 percent of my portfolio to silver even if *none* of the above three indicators were in place. At that point, the inflationary cycle becomes your dominant determinant of how much you invest in silver.

TABLE 7
Silver Statistical Summary, Non-Communist World, 1961–85
(Millions of Troy Ounces)

| | CONSUMPTION | | | | | SECONDARY SUPPLIES | | | | NET |
YEAR	INDUSTRIAL	COINAGE	TOTAL CONSUMPTION	MINE PRODUCTION	PRIMARY DEFICIT	U.S. TREASURY SALES	U.S. TREASURY COINAGE	OTHER SECONDARY SUPPLIES	TOTAL SECONDARY SUPPLIES	SURPLUS (+) DEFICIT (−)*
1961	240	137	377	204	173	63	56	129	248	+75
1962	258	128	386	211	175	1	77	101	179	+4
1963	261	166	427	214	213	25	112	83	220	+7
1964	295	267	562	212	350	151	203	112	466	+116
1965	330	381	711	218	493	80	320	137	537	+44
1966	348	130	478	225	253	143	54	133	330	+77
1967	341	105	446	215	231	195	44	151	390	+159
1968	342	89	431	230	201	180	37	220	437	+236
1969	350	33	383	249	134	89	19	185	293	+159
1970	339	23	362	259	103	67	1	140	208	+105
1971	351	28	379	247	132	0	2	128	130	−2
1972	388	38	426	249	177	0	2	118	120	−57
1973	470	23	493	254	239	0	1	174	175	−64
1974	425	38	463	240	223	0	1	182	183	−40
1975	370	33	403	241	162	0	3	188	191	+29
1976	410	30	440	247	193	0	1	228	229	+36
1977	395	27	422	261	161	0	0	171	171	+10
1978	443	36	479	269	210	0	0	165	165	−45
1979	420	28	448	267	181	0	0	143	143	−38

Year									
1980	350	14	364	255	109	0	227	227	+118
1981	344	9	353	286	67	2	153	155	+88
1982	352	13	365	306	59	3	137	140	+81
1983	350	20	370	316	54	12	140	152	+98
1984	363	9	372	321	51	3	113	116	+65
1985	374	9	383	320	63	0	102	106	+43

*Change in private stocks

Sources: J. Aron Precious Metals Research Department.
1961–1977: Handy & Harman, U.S. Bureau of Mines, the Silver Institute, and private sources.
1978–1985: Handy & Harman, *The Silver Market 1982* and *The Silver Market 1985.*

TABLE 8

Silver Coinage and Secondary U.S. Treasury Supplies,
1961–69 (Millions of Troy Ounces)

YEAR	NON-COMMUNIST COINAGE	SECONDARY SUPPLIES FROM U.S. TREASURY
1961	137	119
1962	128	78
1963	166	137
1964	267	354
1965	381	400
1966	130	197
1967	105	239
1968	89	217
1969	33	108
	1,436	1,849

Source: J. Aron and Handy & Harman.

TABLE 9
Silver's Primary Deficit, Except Coinage and
U.S. Treasury Sales, in Non-Communist World,
1961–85 (Millions of Troy Ounces)

YEAR	INDUSTRIAL CONSUMPTION	MINE PRODUCTION	BASIC GAP	SECONDARY SOURCES	SURPLUS (DEFICIT)
1961	240	204	36	129	93
1962	258	211	47	101	54
1963	261	214	47	83	36
1964	295	212	83	112	29
1965	330	218	112	137	26
1966	348	225	123	133	10
1967	341	215	126	151	25
1968	342	230	112	220	108
1969	350	249	101	185	84
1970	339	259	80	140	60
1971	351	247	104	128	24
1972	388	249	139	118	(11)
1973	470	254	216	174	(42)
1974	425	240	185	182	(3)
1975	370	241	129	188	59
1976	410	247	163	228	65
1977	395	261	134	171	37
1978	443	269	174	165	(9)
1979	420	268	152	143	(9)
1980	350	255	95	227	132
1981	344	286	58	155	97
1982	352	306	46	140	94
1983	350	316	34	152	118
1984	363	321	42	116	74
1985	374	320	54	106	52

Sources: J. Aron, *Silver Statistics,* March 1978.
Handy & Harman, *The Silver Market 1982* and *The Silver Market 1985.*

TABLE 10

Twenty-five Leading Silver-Producing Mines in the United States in 1984, in Order of Output

RANK	MINE	COUNTY AND STATE	OPERATOR	SOURCE OF SILVER
1	Sunshine	Shoshone, ID	Sunshine Mining Co.	Silver ore
2	Lucky Friday	Shoshone, ID	Hecla Mining Co.	Silver ore
3	Troy	Lincoln, MT	ASARCO Incorporated	Silver ore
4	Galena	Shoshone, ID	ASARCO Incorporated	Silver ore
5	Candelaria	Mineral, NV	NERCO, Inc.	Silver ore
6	Coeur	Shoshone, ID	ASARCO Incorporated	Silver ore
7	Escalante	Iron, UT	Hecla Mining Co.	Silver ore
8	DeLamar	Owyhee, ID	NERCO, Inc.	Gold-silver ore
9	Utah Copper (Bingham)	Salt Lake, UT	Kennecott	Copper ore
10	Taylor	White Pine, NV	Silver King Mines, Inc.	Silver ore
11	Black Pine	Granite, MT	Black Pine Mining Co.	Silver ore
12	Bulldog	Mineral, CO	Homestake Mining Co.	Silver ore
13	Tyrone	Grant, NM	Phelps Dodge Corp.	Copper ore
14	Sierrita	Pima, AZ	Duval Corp.	Copper ore
15	Sixteen-to-One	Esmeralda, NV	Sunshine Mining Co.	Silver ore
16	Morenci	Greenlee, AZ	Phelps Dodge Corp.	Copper ore
17	Crescent	Shoshone, ID	Bunker Limited Partnership	Silver ore
18	Gooseberry	Storey, NV	Asamera Minerals (U.S.), Inc.	Gold-silver ore
19	Buick	Iron, MO	AMAX Lead Co. of Missouri	Lead ore

20	Eisenhower	Pima, AZ	Eisenhower Mining Co.	Copper ore
21	San Manuel	Pinal, AZ	Magma Copper Co.	Copper ore
22	St. Cloud	Sierra, NM	St. Cloud Mining Co.	Silver ore
23	Ray	Pinal, AZ	Kennecott	Copper ore
24	Battle Mountain	Lander, NV	Duval Corp.	Gold ore
25	Magmont	Iron, MO	Cominco American Incorporated	Lead ore

Source: U.S. Department of the Interior, Bureau of Mines, *Minerals Yearbook, 1984*, Vol. 1, *Metals and Minerals*, "Silver," Table 4, p. 818.

TABLE 11
U.S. Consumption of Silver by End-Use, 1974–85 (Thousands of Troy Ounces)

	1974	1975	1976	1977	1978	1979	1980	1981	1982	1983	1984	1985
Electroplated ware	13.2	8.7	9.5	6.8	7.3	8.1	4.4	3.9	3.4	3.2	3.5	3.9
Sterling ware	22.1	23.7	19.8	16.7	17.9	13.0	9.1	4.4	7.8	7.0	3.6	3.6
Jewelry	5.2	12.7	10.9	8.1	6.8	5.3	5.9	5.4	6.4	6.9	5.8	5.5
Photographic materials	49.5	46.1	55.5	53.7	64.3	66.0	49.8	51.0	52.1	51.8	55.3	58.0
Dental and medical supplies	2.4	1.5	1.9	2.2	2.0	2.3	2.2	1.7	1.7	1.5	1.5	1.5
Mirrors	3.9	3.2	4.6	2.1	1.9	1.9	.7	.6	1.0	1.0	1.0	1.0
Brazing alloys and solders	14.5	13.6	11.2	12.6	11.0	10.9	8.5	7.7	6.3	5.8	5.9	5.8
Elec/electronic products												
Batteries	4.2	4.3	3.5	5.8	6.0	4.6	6.0	3.8	4.4	2.6	2.7	2.7
Contacts, conductors	31.3	27.2	32.3	31.3	30.8	33.5	27.8	26.4	28.7	26.3	25.6	27.0
Bearings	.4	.5	.3	.5	.4	.3	.6	.3	.3	.2	.3	.2
Catalysts	7.3	8.8	12.3	8.9	8.2	5.6	3.0	3.8	2.4	2.4	2.4	2.5
Coins, medallions, common objects	22.2	7.1	8.2	4.3	2.7	4.7	4.6	2.6	3.4	3.0	2.6	2.3
Miscellaneous*	.5	.3	.3	.9	.9	1.0	2.1	5.0	4.4	4.6	4.6	4.6
Total Consumption	177.0	157.7	170.6	153.8	160.2	157.2	124.7	116.6	122.3	116.3	114.8	118.6

Sources: J. Aron, Silver Statistics and Analysis, March 1978; Handy & Harman, The Silver Market 1982 and The Silver Market 1985.
*Includes silver-bearing copper, silver-bearing lead anodes, ceramic paints, etc.

Where to Buy Silver

My recommendations here are basically the same as for buying gold, so you may want to review the section on dealers in Chapter 3. Here I will just highlight a few of the most highly recommended dealers.

Rhode Island Hospital Trust National Bank
One Hospital Trust Plaza
Providence, RI 02903-2449
  Telephones (800) 942-2409 and (401) 278-8496

Hospital Trust has silver bullion available in bars of 1 ounce, 10 ounces, and 100 ounces. The minimum silver purchase is 50 ounces.

Benham Certified Metals
755 Page Mill Road
Palo Alto, CA 94304
  Telephone (800) 447-GOLD

Benham Certified Metals can offer you 90 percent silver bags, as well as silver bars in a variety of sizes and weights. The minimum transaction amount for silver is $1,000.

Manfra, Tordella and Brookes, Inc.
30 Rockefeller Plaza
New York, NY 10012
  Telephones (800) 223-5818 and (212) 621-9500

MTB sells silver in all of the usual forms: 90 percent bags, individual coins, and bullion bars. Ask for their booklet, "Silver—Investing In and Collecting Silver Bars and Coinage."

Finally, Hecla Mining Co. is an excellent silver stock to purchase on a dollar cost averaging basis. Hecla is America's number one primary-silver producer, with over 8 million ounces of silver mined in 1984. It owns the Lucky Friday mine as well as the Escalante Mine in Utah, the crown jewel of its Ranchers Exploration acquisitions.

· FIVE ·

The Right Mix for Your Financial Coat of Armor

In Part I, I have been considering only the defensive part of your Financial Armadillo Strategy—your "coat of armor," which consists of Treasury securities, gold, and possibly silver. Later I will show you how to divide your available funds between these defensive investments designed to protect your principal (your coat of armor) and the aggressive investments that dig for profits (your "sharp claws"). For now, let's figure out the right mix for your coat of armor.

First we must determine which U.S. Treasury note offers the best opportunity, given yield and maturity. To find the current rates, simply turn to the financial pages of a newspaper. In the *Wall Street Journal,* look for the listing with the headline, "Treasury Issues/Bonds, Notes and Bills." In *The New York Times,* the heading is "Treasury Bills, Bonds and Notes." In *Barron's,* look for the page headlined "Government Bonds," in the "Market Week" section at the back of each issue.

We examine the current yields on one-year to seven-year Treasury notes to select the issue with the best yield and maturity characteristics. Table 12 presents this information as it stands while I write. You will want to compile the same type of chart, supplying current figures but otherwise following the steps I give you.

The final column of the table, "Yield Gain from Prior Year," is the crux of the matter, and will require some simple subtraction on your part. All the rest comes from the newspaper.

In this instance, the six-year Treasury note is your best bet. Beyond this point, the gain in yield is modest when related to the necessity of having to hold a piece of paper with a longer maturity. I consistently find that the "best bet" maturity ranges

TABLE 12
Treasury Notes

YEARS (No.)	RATE (%)	MATURITY	YIELD (%)	YIELD GAIN FROM PRIOR YEAR (%)
1	12⅜	August 1987	5.38	—
2	15⅜	October 1988	6.01	+0.63
3	13⅜	August 1989	6.44	+0.43
4	10¾	August 1990	6.63	+0.19
5	14⅞	August 1991	6.79	+0.16
6	9¾	October 1992	6.96	+0.17
7	11⅞	August 1993	7.08	+0.12

between one and seven years, depending on the stage of the economic cycle.

Your next task is to put together a mix of Treasury notes and gold that provides a current return equal to the ninety-day Treasury bill rate. This mixture will have a very interesting bonus hedge, however (more about that in a moment).

Why do I want a return that is equal to the yield on ninety-day Treasury bills? Because they're the benchmark by which I compare the performance of all other assets. The yield on a ninety-day T-bill is somewhat lower than that on a note, but that's because of its very short maturity. Let's face it: Inflation isn't going to pull any great surprise in ninety days if you have been doing your homework. That's why I call the ninety-day Treasury bill a "risk-free" investment benchmark. If I'm going to invest in anything else, it has to offer me significantly greater potential return in exchange for the added risk.

Now, follow my steps closely.

Step 1

I determine the current yield on the ninety-day Treasury bill. As I write, it's 5.30 percent. That means that $100,000 (for example) placed in ninety-day T-bills will provide a return of $5,300 twelve months later.

Step 2

I determine what percentage of my "best-bet" note's yield could be obtained by investing in the ninety-day T-bill. To do that, I divide the yield for my best-bet note into the yield for the ninety-day bill.

In this example, the equation is as follows:

$$5.30 \text{ (the T-bill rate)} \div 6.96 \text{ (the T-note rate)} = .7615 \text{ (76.15 percent)}$$

The ninety-day Treasury bill's return, in other words, is 76.15 percent of the yield from the six-year Treasury note. Therefore, $76,150 invested at 6.96 percent interest provides approximately the same yield as $100,000 invested at the T-bill rate of 5.30 percent (annualized basis).

Step 3 (the bonus hedge)

After investing 76 percent of my $100,000 in six-year Treasury notes, I place the remaining 24 percent ($23,850 in this case) into gold. As I write, the current market price of gold is approximately $385 per ounce, so my $23,850 will purchase approximately 62 ounces of gold. I buy this in the form of gold coins or certificates, *not* gold shares.

This gold doesn't earn me interest, of course. But with this mixture—approximately 76 percent of my assets in six-year Treasury notes and 24 percent in gold—my overall yield is still equal to the yield on the "risk-free" investment, the ninety-day Treasury bill. We have locked in a guaranteed 5.30 percent yield for six years. This is a yield, moreover, that is free of state and local taxes.

Now let's look at exactly what this means in terms of the benefits of the Financial Armadillo Strategy. This strategy provides you with (1) *real* profits that outpace inflation, (2) absolute safety of principal, (3) a safety net against potential price inflation, and (4) similar protection against potential price deflation.

Let's take a quick look at each of those benefits in turn.

Real Profits that Outpace Inflation

With a locked-in, guaranteed yield of 5.30 percent for six years, we are 3.8 percent ahead of current inflation. And that's assuming *no* appreciation in the value of your gold during those six years.

Absolute Safety of Principal

Your Financial Armadillo's coat of armor consists of the two most solid investments available to anyone. Your Treasury notes are backed by the full power and force of the U.S. government. Gold has held its value over the centuries. Even if the next six years see lower gold prices, however, the 76 percent weighting in favor of Treasury securities assures you absolute safety of principal.

A Safety Net Against Potential
Price Inflation

In any period of surging inflation, your rather sizable 24-percent gold position should be more than enough to offset the reduced value of your Treasury notes. We noted in our charts how the price of gold tends to exceed the rise in price inflation by a hefty margin. Also, remember that you are holding your Treasury notes only for a limited period of time. It's comforting to know that at the end of six years the U.S. government stands ready to redeem your notes, and you don't have to be concerned about a non-liquid market.

A Safety Net Against
Potential Price Deflation

In a period of actual consumer price deflation, the price of gold would most likely—but by no means definitely—decline. But gold represents only 24 percent of the Financial Armadillo's coat of armor. Any decline in that part of the package would be more than offset by the appreciation of the 76 percent invested in Treasury notes. The purchasing power of their fixed yield would be enhanced as goods and services are offered in the marketplace at reduced prices. With this mix, it matters not at all what happens to the value of gold during those six years.

There you have it. For safety and growth of your long-range financial insurance policy, you could hardly ask for more than you get from the Financial Armadillo's coat of armor. Sleep soundly tonight!

And may I now call you "my fellow armadillo"?

· Part II ·

THE FINANCIAL ARMADILLO'S SHARP CLAWS— DIGGING FOR PROFITS

· SIX ·

Mutual Funds

In this section, we will look at some of the Financial Armadillo's "sharp claws." While the armadillo's coat of armor provides the protection you need in your investment program, the claws dig for profits. To make certain those profits are as large as possible, you must also utilize the Financial Armadillo's survival instinct—a keen sense of timing. I'll show you how to develop that sense of timing in Part III: Chapters 9 and 10 will tell you *when* to use your claws, and when *not* to. But for now let's look at the claws themselves, starting with one of the most common and useful financial instruments available to investors today: mutual funds.

How Mutual Funds Can Turn You
into a Professional Investor

Good investment analysis is a complex undertaking. Advanced skills in accounting and quantitative studies are essential today. Beyond having those skills, one must be a seasoned veteran within a particular industry in order to comprehend what really makes a company in a given field tick. The ability to size up corporate leaders is also vital. A strong leader has turned many a weak company around and confounded the "experts."

Today a first-rate securities analyst is both scientist and artist. People skills are often as vital to success as academic skills. First-rate analysts can follow only a single industry or a small group of non-industrial companies. It becomes essential to forge a team, which means knowing how to pick specialists in other major industry groupings.

Competition is keen, and there is no room for an average analyst. Wall Street's best analysts earn upwards of $500,000 per year, and salaries of $100,000 are commonplace. The best analysts are often those who have served a long apprenticeship in a particular industry. The best computer industry analyst will, no doubt, be an individual who has had significant experience working in that industry.

Gideon Gartner is a perfect example. He spent ten years in the computer industry, primarily with IBM, where he had worldwide responsibility for its intelligence-gathering operation. Then he turned to a successful career on Wall Street before forming his prestigious Gartner Group, Inc., based in Stamford, Connecticut.

The average weekend investor cannot compete with a Gideon Gartner. In fact, ninety-nine percent of the professionals on Wall Street cannot compete with Gartner's experience and expertise.

We have just covered one of the best reasons to make mutual funds a cornerstone of your investment program.

1. *Mutual funds provide professional management.* You have your own life and your own career. Concentrate on handling that well, and rely on fulltime professionals to make the complex decisions of which companies and which stocks will do well.

2. *Mutual funds save you valuable time.* Even if you have the ability to become a good securities analyst, do you really want to take the time? It's more than a fulltime job in itself. Realistically, most investors have just a few hours a week, at most, to devote to their investments. Better to spend that time on analysis that will make *all* your investments more productive. Spend just an hour or so a week determining where you stand in the business cycle (I'll show you how in Chapter 9) and what the future course of inflation will be (I'll show you how to do *that* in Chapter 10). Leave the time-consuming stock selections to mutual fund professionals with a proven track record (and I'll show you how to pick *them* in a few pages).

3. *Mutual funds provide diversification.* First of all, as we'll see, mutual fund "families" offer you a portfolio mix that includes the stock market, money fund or short-term Treasury securities, and an inflation-hedging position. Second, an individual fund will offer you diversification within its area. A stock market fund, for example, will have a wide range of stock investments. Over the long run, diversification is always wise insurance— you're not putting all your investment eggs in one basket.

4. *Mutual funds offer an easy and orderly way to invest.* This

is certainly not a speculative approach, but one geared for the investor with long-term goals in mind. Good information is available on the funds (I'll show you where), and the funds themselves are easy to purchase. You don't have to worry about salespeople putting pressure on you to invest.

5. *Mutual funds help you in your tax paperwork.* Most fund groups provide excellent detailed statements on a monthly, quarterly, and annual basis. Year-end statements provide all the tax information you or your accountant will require.

6. *Most important of all, the mutual fund approach works.* Over the past ten years, the average equities (stock) mutual fund has outpaced the popular market indices (such as the S&P 500) consistently.

Of course, mutual fund performances are not uniform. In fact, they range from the dismal to the sublime, as with any type of investment vehicle. Also, there are so many funds available today that picking the right ones is a good deal more time-consuming and difficult than it was just five years ago. Let's look at some guidelines for making the right decisions.

Ten Ways to Profit from Mutual Funds

1. Get Your Money's Worth

Mutual funds can be divided into two basic categories: load and no-load.

Load funds are sold through stockbrokers, financial planners, insurance companies, and some independent mutual fund organizations. They have a sales charge ranging from 8.5 percent of the dollar value of your investment (the legal maximum) down to 1 or 2 percent ("low-load"). The sales charge can be deducted at the time of purchase ("front-end load") or when you sell your shares ("back-end load"). Either way you are paying a commission to the sales organization. For example, if you invest $1,000 in an 8.5 percent front-end-load fund, $85 goes to the salesperson and only $915 actually buys shares in the fund.

No-load mutual funds have no sales charge. A $1,000 investment buys you $1,000 worth of the fund's shares. No-load mutual funds usually use space advertisements in financial publications or direct mail to reach their customers directly.

Load funds justify their sales charge by claiming they perform better for you—that you will make more money with them, even after you deduct the sales commissions. However, extensive studies indicate that there is no correlation between sales charges and performance. In short, load funds *on the average* do not perform any better than no-load funds. This tips the scales rather convincingly in favor of no-load funds. Remember this when you are approached by a mutual fund salesperson.

Today there is a trend for top-performing no-loads to add a 1 percent to 3 percent sales charge to new shareholder purchases. Thus the no-load becomes a low-load. Although I feel sales charges are an unnecessary burden, one could argue that consistent superior performance justifies the small sales charge.

When looking into a fund, always determine in advance exactly what fees and commissions, if any, will be levied. Then look into the fund's performance record to see if you think this cost is justified.

2. Buy a Mutual Fund Designed to Satisfy Your Financial Needs and Objectives

Although there are endless ways to classify mutual funds by investment objectives, the most common classifications are income funds, growth funds, and aggressive growth funds. These are three very different animals.

As the name implies, *income funds* are designed to provide income for investors who need it. Income funds invest in high-yielding securities (usually a mix of stocks and bonds) and pass the yield on to fund shareholders via quarterly dividend distributions. Capital appreciation is a secondary objective and tends not to be a major part of the total return picture. Although some income funds—such as Fidelity Equity-Income (2 percent load) and Evergreen Total Return Fund (no-load)—have exceptional performance records, they are rarely at the top of the performance charts. These are generally conservative investments oriented toward capital preservation, and thus are for persons who are interested in protecting their savings while earning income.

Growth funds, the most popular type of mutual fund, are designed to produce long-term capital appreciation for shareholders. Although some growth funds will distribute dividend income periodically, most will reinvest dividends in their port-folios. Growth funds buy stocks of all shapes and sizes, but the staple is established growth companies with consistent above-average earnings records. Growth funds are ideal investments for people attempting to "grow" assets over the long term—to pay for a child's college education or to prepare financially for retirement. Fidelity Magellan Fund (3 percent load) and the Nicholas Fund (no-load) are good examples of traditional growth funds.

Aggressive growth funds are the high flyers of the mutual fund industry. These funds invest in small, speculative stocks. Performance is volatile, soaring in bull markets and free-falling in down markets. A good one will have a long-term perfor-mance record that is above the market average, despite these sharp short-term swings. Nevertheless, aggressive growth funds are not for timid investors or those who may need to sell shares to raise money at inappropriate times, such as major bear mar-kets. Hartwell Growth Fund and Hartwell Leverage Fund are classic aggressive growth funds.

An important note of caution: Do not be seduced by any aggressive growth fund's short-term performance record. Just because it was up 100 percent in a big bull market doesn't mean it will double again in the next twelve months. More than a few unwary mutual fund investors have been burned by buying ag-gressive growth funds at market tops.

Some mutual funds cannot be classified easily in these three categories. The no-load Lehman Capital Fund, for example, is a hybrid fund which blends the characteristics of a straight growth fund and an aggressive growth fund. The no-load Mutual Shares is another example of a hybrid fund. It performs like a classic growth fund, but invests primarily in value stocks.

3. Check the Performance Record, but Don't Be Deceived by It

"Past performance does not necessarily reflect future prospects" is a standard disclaimer on all the investment industry's promo-tional literature. While I recognize that the past is not neces-sarily a prologue to the future of any investment, I do believe a mutual fund's past performance record is the single best criteria for determining its likely future performance. Barring a change in management or a dramatic upheaval in the financial markets, mutual funds that have consistently outperformed the competition and the averages are more likely to continue to do so than those that haven't. This is plain old-fashioned common sense.

So, the first step in choosing a mutual fund is to look at the record. In my opinion, the key performance measurement is *average annual total return* (capital appreciation and dividends reinvested or distributed) over a period encompassing at least one bull market and one bear market. Focusing on average annual total return over a full market cycle helps you avoid funds that give up most of their bull-market gains during periods when the market is declining.

Remember that statistics can lie, and mutual fund promoters are not above using numbers to shed a favorable light on their funds' performance over a selected period that just happens to coincide with good stock market years. A good example is an aggressive growth fund touting its 1982–83 record. Another deceptive technique is to stretch the record to include a few phenomenal years in the fund's early history. One famous growth fund highlights an impressive fifteen-year record in its sales literature to disguise the fact that the fund hasn't even kept pace with the market averages in any of the last seven years.

The moral of this story is check the record, but do not get fooled by selectively isolated performance statistics.

Now, where will you find the statistics? *Forbes* and *Barron's* publish mutual fund performance reviews, which are excellent tools for mutual fund investors. *Forbes'* annual fund review, published every September, focuses on average annual total return over the last ten years. The *Barron's* quarterly mutual fund reviews concentrate on five-year performance statistics. *Forbes* also grades funds "A" to "F" for their performances in bull markets and their performances in bear markets. Its special honor roll consists of those funds earning a "B" or better in both bull and bear markets. This honor roll is perhaps your best shopping list of funds worthy of consideration.

Many other publications and services review mutual fund performances in greater depth. Of course they also cost more than the *Forbes* or *Barron's* mutual fund review issues. As you become more experienced or have more to invest, you may want to consult one of the following:

Sheldon Jacob's *Handbook for No-Load Fund Investors* is

my personal favorite. It is available for $29.00 from Box 283, Hastings-on-Hudson, NY 10706.

William E. Donoghue's No-Load Mutual Fund Guide is the best-selling classic that has probably introduced more small investors to the funds than any other single source. It is available at bookstores in a $3.50 Bantam Books paperback edition.

And if you join the American Association of Individual Investors (recommended in Chapter 12) you can get *The Individual Investor's Guide to No-Load Mutual Funds*. For information write to the Association at 612 North Michigan Avenue, Chicago, IL 60611.

4. Know Who's Boss

A mutual fund is only as good as its manager. Funds with superior long-term records often perform poorly after a talented portfolio manager leaves. This is particularly true in smaller funds managed by just one person. When researching a mutual fund, therefore, make certain it is being run by the person or persons who are responsible for its good past record. This information can be found in any mutual fund prospectus. If you cannot find it there, or if the language seems evasive, ask the fund to advise you in writing who the portfolio managers are, and how long they have held that responsibility.

5. Beware of Funds that Have Grown Too Fast

Young companies often experience growing pains when their business becomes larger and more complicated. The same thing tends to happen with mutual funds. The classic example is the small growth fund which, due to its impressive performance record, becomes a big fund almost overnight. The fund manager who was comfortable managing a relatively small portfolio of stocks may not be able to do as well with a much bigger portfolio. Be wary, therefore, of the $50 million mutual fund that becomes a $200 million fund in just one or two years. Its performance is likely to deteriorate.

6. Avoid New Funds

New mutual funds tend to be introduced near market peaks because it is easiest to sell mutual fund shares when interest in the market is most intense. It is not unusual to see the value of such a new fund's shares drop sharply in the year after its formation. In addition, unless the new fund is being managed by someone with a discernible track record, the past performance criteria so essential in evaluating a mutual fund are not available.

These first six points should help you in your efforts to select a profitable mutual fund. The next four points will suggest strategies you can use in a comprehensive mutual fund investment program.

7. Specialty Funds: Playing Special Segments of the Market

Specialty funds have become very popular in recent years. Today you can buy mutual funds investing exclusively in industries ranging from high technology to utilities or gold mining.

By definition, there is little or no diversification by industry in specialty funds. They should not, therefore, be used as core holdings in a comprehensive mutual fund investment program. That role should be filled by one or two growth funds for growth-oriented investors or several income funds for those desiring yield.

As your investments increase in size and range, however, you can devote a portion of your investment assets to specialty funds in industries you believe to have particularly bright prospects. If, for example, you feel medical technology will be an exceptional growth industry in the next several years, you may want to put a small percentage of your total investment money in a specialized med-tech fund. Similarly, if you think gold is ready to run, you may want to buy a few shares in a gold fund.

I believe investing in specialty mutual funds is a safer way to play an industry group than buying one or two individual stocks within the group. If you pick the right group at the right time, you can receive some very special profits.

8. The Family of Funds: Mutual Fund Investing Made Easy

Some of the larger mutual fund organizations offer "families" of funds that include conventional growth and income funds as well as specialty funds. A money market fund is usually part of the family package, along with telephone switching privileges permitting investors to shift assets between the funds with just a phone call. A family of funds is the ultimate in one-step mutual fund shopping.

In selecting a mutual fund family, you should look for one having at least two growth funds—an income fund and a money market fund—and, for the more adventuresome, aggressive growth and specialty funds. The majority of the funds should be no-loads or low-loads. Check the past performance records of all the equity (stock) funds to insure that it is a successful family, not a group of losers. Make certain the telephone switching privilege is available, check the costs (some fund families charge fees for telephone switching), and see if there are any limitations on the switching privilege.

If you are an investor who follows my advice and participates in the stock market only during advances, sitting on the sidelines during declines, the family-of-funds approach makes for hassle-free mutual fund investing. Use the money market fund as a safe haven for your money when you expect a broad market dip, and then shift into equity funds when the stock market looks like the place to be.

A word of caution about this strategy: The stock market can often fool even the most highly trained observers. Avoid short-term trading and look for broad cyclical changes in the market. If you get fooled consistently, your investment performance probably will not match a simple buy-and-hold strategy. The way to avoid being fooled is to pay special attention to Chapter 9, "What the Financial Armadillo Must Know About the Business Cycle."

Some of my recommendations for mutual fund families will follow in a few pages.

9. International Funds: A Safer Way to Invest in Foreign Markets

Analyzing foreign securities is even more difficult than researching domestic stocks. Accounting principles vary from country to country, making standard U.S. investment yardsticks inappropriate. Foreign markets often respond to local economic situations that most American investors may not be aware of. Consequently, investing in foreign markets is best left to the professional.

Fortunately, there are mutual funds specializing in foreign

securities. These allow the amateur to participate in foreign markets with professional and specialized guidance. The no-load T. Rowe Price International Fund and the no-load Scudder International Fund are typical funds specializing in foreign securities.

While most foreign markets have lagged behind the U.S. market in the 1980s, they outperformed the U.S. market through much of the 1970s. Should the tables turn again, international funds may prove to be very profitable investments. A small position in an international fund may also help hedge against major U.S. bear markets.

10. The Closed-End Fund: A Golden Opportunity

Thus far we have been discussing open-end mutual funds. These funds continually issue and redeem shares upon demand. Typically, if you invest $1,000, you are issued one thousand "shares" in the fund, and the fund becomes as big as the demand for it.

Closed-end mutual funds, on the other hand, issue a fixed number of shares, which then trade like stocks on the securities exchanges. When you buy a closed-end fund, you are getting professional management and a diversified portfolio, just as you are when you buy a conventional open-end fund. When you want to buy or sell shares in a closed-end fund, you must do so through a broker and pay a commission.

I mention closed-end funds here because one in particular happens to be arguably the best way to play a bull market in gold. ASA Ltd., a closed-end fund which trades on the New York Stock Exchange, owns a portfolio of South African gold shares (gold mine stocks). These gold shares have a volatile reaction to changes in the price of gold—they soar when gold goes up, and sink when the price of gold declines. For example, in January 1985, when the price of gold was down .3 percent, ASA dropped 7.3 percent. And in March 1985, when gold climbed 8.9 percent, ASA was up 14.7 percent.

If you have the golden touch in forecasting the future price of gold, ASA can be the most profitable way to play. To help you get that golden touch, pay special attention to Chapter 3 ("Gold") and to Chapter 10 ("What the Financial Armadillo Must Know About Inflation").

My Three Favorite "Families"
of Mutual Funds

The number of mutual fund "families" has grown along with the number of individual funds. Here are my three favorite ones:

1. Vanguard Group
   Vanguard Financial Center
   Valley Forge, PA 19482
   (800) 362-0530 (local)
   (800) 662-7447 (out of state)

I have kept a close watch on the Vanguard Group of mutual funds for over fifteen years, and utilize them in the investment portfolios I manage. This family has now expanded to nearly three dozen funds and portfolios, with more than $13.5 billion in net assets and over 800,000 shareholder accounts.

Vanguard's star performers have been the Explorer Fund, which has appeared on *Forbes'* exclusive "honor roll" of top-performing funds, and the Windsor Fund. For the 1976–1985 period, both stock funds outperformed the S&P 500 by a hefty margin. Average annual growth of the S&P 500 during that period was 12.5 percent. During the same years, average annual total return was 20.7 percent for the Explorer Fund and 19.4 percent for the Windsor Fund.

Unfortunately, both of these funds proved so popular and grew so large that Vanguard closed them to new accounts in May 1985. Their successors promise to follow the same methods that brought success to the parent funds, but of course you must regularly monitor their performance to make certain they do. I am a big fan of Vanguard's head, John C. Bogle, and feel his selection of investment advisors for the new funds will work out well.

John Neff has managed the Windsor Fund for years. He popularized the contrary opinion approach to stock selection and emphasizes stocks with low price-to-earnings ratios (see Chapter 7). Windsor II, managed by Barrow, Hanley, McWhinney, and Strauss, promises to follow "a value-oriented 'growth and income' investment strategy like its forerunner, Windsor Fund." Specifically, says Vanguard, Windsor II seeks *long-term growth of*

capital and income through an investment approach emphasizing income-producing common stocks with:
 • Price-to-earnings ratios lower than the market.
 • Price-to-book values lower than the market.
 • Dividend yields higher than the market.

Windsor II invests in stocks considered by the portfolio manager to be undervalued at the time of purchase. In other words, the marketplace has not yet "priced" the stocks commensurate with their underlying *fundamental value,* as measured by:
 • earnings and revenues
 • industry position
 • management expertise
 • growth potential.

The Explorer Fund emphasizes investments in high-tech stocks of relatively small, embryonic companies. Its excellent results have been obtained by manager Frank Wisneski. Explorer II promises to continue this tradition under the direction of another highly respected investment advisor, John J. Granahan. As the principal of Granahan Investment Management, he has been researching, analyzing, and managing small company growth portfolios for more than twenty-five years.

"The investment objective of Explorer II," says Vanguard,

> is to achieve *maximum growth of capital over the long term by investing in common stocks of small, unseasoned, or embryonic companies. . . .*
>
> Explorer II invests in carefully researched companies and managements, not in tips and rumors. Its timetable is based not on days, weeks, or months, but on *years.*
>
> What's more, you get the diversification and liquidity that is critical when investing in small, thinly traded growth stocks. Such features simply are not available when you purchase Explorer II-type equities directly . . . provided you can buy them at all.

This last point is critically important. Small high-tech companies offer great growth potential for investors—everyone wants to be in on the ground floor of "the next Xerox" or "the next IBM." But they also offer much higher risk than blue-chip stocks, as business headlines attest every day. A good mutual fund is the best and safest way to spread your risk and still enjoy the rapid growth potential of these stocks.

This also applies to Vanguard's specialized portfolios in energy, health care, gold and precious metals, the service economy, and technology. Other funds specialize in growth stocks, stocks and bonds, municipal bonds, corporate bonds, and money market instruments. The family of funds has something for every stock market environment and investment objective. See Table 13 for Vanguard's profile of its funds and Table 14 for their cumulative performance records.

Vanguard offers IRA plans, Keogh plans for self-employed individuals, 403 plans for employees of educational or tax-exempt organizations, and 401(k) money purchase and profit-sharing plans for corporate employee benefit plans. Vanguard Discount Brokerage Services offers savings of up to 70 percent on the purchase of individual stocks, bonds, and options. This is, indeed, a major "supermarket" of financial services.

2. T. Rowe Price Associates
   100 East Pratt Street
   Baltimore, MD 21202
   (301) 547-2308 (local)
   (800) 638-5660 (out of state)

This is another excellent family of mutual funds. I have been involved with the group for well over a decade and have found its management to be outstanding.

T. Rowe Price has Treasury and money market funds, as well as funds specializing in municipal bonds, bonds and preferred stocks, and stocks of all kinds, including its International Fund. Its Prime Reserve Fund is one of the highest yielding money market funds available, and the stock funds include two rated "A" by *Forbes* for bull markets—New Era and New Horizons. The S&P 500 grew by an average annual rate of 12.5 percent between 1976 and 1985. During that period, the New Era Fund had an average annual total return of 15.1 percent, and the New Horizons Fund figure was 18.0 percent.

The New Era Fund invests primarily in companies whose earnings and/or value of tangible assets are expected to grow faster than the rate of inflation over the long term. During periods of high inflation, it tends to invest in natural resources

TABLE 13
A Profile of Vanguard No-Load Mutual Funds

INVESTMENT OBJECTIVE	INVESTMENT POLICY	POTENTIAL CAPITAL APPRECIATION	STABILITY OF INCOME	STABILITY OF PRINCIPAL	VANGUARD FUND/PORTFOLIO	MINIMUM INITIAL INVESTMENT[1]
Maximum capital growth	Aggressive growth stocks	Very high	Low	Very low	Explorer II	$3,000
					Naess & Thomas	3,000
					Vanguard Specialized Portfolios:	
					• Energy	1,500
					• Health Care	1,500
					• Gold & Precious Metals	1,500
					• Service Economy	1,500
					• Technology	1,500
Capital appreciation	Growth stocks	High	Moderate	Low	Ivest Fund	1,500
					W. L. Morgan Growth Fund	1,500
Income and capital growth	Growth and income stocks	High	Tends to grow	Low to moderate	Windsor II	1,500
					Vanguard Index Trust	1,500
Current income and conservation of capital	Stocks and bonds	Moderate	Grows modestly	Moderate	Wellington Fund	1,500
					Wellesley Income Fund	1,500
					Vanguard STAR Fund	500

						Minimum
Tax-free income	Municipal bonds[2]	Moderate	Moderate to high	Low to moderate	Vanguard Municipal Bond Fund: • Money Market • Short-Term • Intermediate-Term • Long-Term • High-Yield • Insured Long-Term	3,000 3,000 3,000 3,000 3,000 3,000
Current income	Short-term corporate bonds	Low	High	Moderate	Vanguard Short-Term Bond	3,000
Current income	Long-term bonds	Moderate	High	Low to moderate	Vanguard Fixed Income Securities Fund: • Investment-Grade Bond • High-Yield Bond • GNMA	3,000 3,000 3,000
Current income plus capital protection	Money market instruments	None	Low	Very high	Vanguard Money Market Trust: • Prime • Federal • Insured	1,000 1,000 1,000

[1]These minimums will be waived for tax-deferred plans, including IRA, profit sharing, and pension plans.
[2]Not suitable for retirement plans.

stocks—companies that will benefit from rising raw materials prices—and other companies where management has the flexibility to adjust prices or the ability to control operating costs. Whenever inflation begins to rise and you are looking for an inflation-oriented fund, there is none better than New Era.

T. Rowe Price's New Horizons Fund is one of the better funds in the country for investing in small, rapidly growing companies. Its largest segment of holdings is with high-technology companies—electronics, instrumentation, medicine, data processing, communications, and devices that result in labor savings or productivity improvement. It also looks for companies in the massive service sector of the economy—"imaginative companies which can offer new or improved goods or services to consumers, business, and government." And in the consumer sector it has found specialty retailing to be a large and profitable area of investment—companies that innovate (such as off-price retailing), develop new markets (such as consumer electronics), or simply operate more efficiently.

T. Rowe Price has a full array of services such as IRAs, 401(k) plans, and discount brokerage services.

3. Neuberger & Berman Management
   342 Madison Avenue
   New York, NY 10173
   (212) 850-8300 (local)
   (800) 367-0770 (out of state)

My third favorite family is smaller than the first two, with only eight mutual funds, but they include some interesting and profitable selections.

Neuberger & Berman's Government Money Fund invests only in Treasury securities and other securities backed by the "full faith and credit" of the U.S. government. Its Liberty Fund takes an aggressive approach to income investing, with high-yielding securities that also carry higher than normal risk. And its Energy Fund is worth your investigation when you think oil stocks are a good buy, such as in a period of rising inflation.

Of Neuberger & Berman's five stock funds, two have outperformed the S&P 500 by considerable margins. Between 1976 and 1985, the S&P 500 had an average annual rise of 12.5 percent. During that same period, Neuberger & Berman's Partners Fund enjoyed an average annual total return of 20.6 percent, with average annual total returns of 17.1 percent earned by the Guardian Mutual Fund. Partners is a capital growth fund, with a higher portfolio turnover rate than other mutual funds and a substantial portion of its portfolio in securities selected for their short-term gain potential. The Partners Fund does particularly well in bear markets, earning an "A" from *Forbes* for performance in down markets (compared with a "C" in up markets). Guardian is more even, earning a "B" from *Forbes* in both up and down markets.

Guardian Mutual Fund is a broad-based common stock fund with a good record that should appeal to conservative investors. It is highly diversified in its holdings, and its record has been improving over the years. Founded in 1950, it has outperformed the S&P 500 in twenty-one of thirty-four full years, including nine of the ten most recent years.

TABLE 14

Cumulative Performance* of Vanguard No-Load Mutual Funds (Periods Ending December 31, 1984)

VANGUARD FUND/PORTFOLIO	1 YEAR	3 YEARS	5 YEARS	10 YEARS
Explorer II	—**	—	—	—
Naess & Thomas Vanguard Specialized Portfolios:	−25.2%	29.5%	81.2%	325.3%
• Energy	− 6.6**	—	—	—
• Health Care	6.6**	—	—	—
• Gold & Precious Metals	−32.7**	—	—	—
• Service Economy	15.6**	—	—	—
• Technology	3.1**	—	—	—
Invest Fund	0.1	49.6	98.1	311.3
W. L. Morgan Growth Fund	− 6.1	54.0	97.5	412.7
Windsor II	—**	—	—	—
Vanguard Index Trust	6.2	55.8	94.9	—
Wellington Fund	10.7	70.4	114.7	279.5
Wellesley Income Fund	16.6	70.6	107.4	244.6

	1 YEAR	3 YEARS	5 YEARS	10 YEARS
Vanguard STAR				
Fund	—**	—	—	—
Vanguard Municipal Bond Fund:				
• Money Market	6.0	19.1	—	—
• Short-Term	6.8	23.6	40.9	—
• Intermediate-Term	9.5	52.9	26.9	—
• Long-Term	8.6	64.7	22.9	—
• High-Yield	9.7	64.5	33.0	—
• Insured Long-Term	—**	—	—	—
Vanguard Short-				
Term Bond	14.2	—	—	—
Vanguard Fixed Income Securities Fund:				
• Investment-Grade				
Bond	14.1	56.8	78.7	141.3
• High-Yield Bond	7.9	58.3	79.1	—
• GNMA	14.0	64.5	—	—
Vanguard Money Market Trust:				
• Prime	10.6	35.8	80.2	—
• Federal	10.2	33.6	—	—
• Insured	9.8	—	—	—

INDEXES	1 YEAR	3 YEARS	5 YEARS	10 YEARS
S&P 500 Index	6.2%	58.0%	99.1%	295.9%
Salomon High Grade				
Bond Index	16.4	75.1	68.9	123.6
Municipal Bond Buyer				
Index	8.8	71.7	24.7	67.3
Lipper Non-Govern-				
ment Money Market	10.2	34.6	77.7	—
Lipper Government				
Money Market	9.7	32.5	—	—

*Total return includes the reinvestment of all income dividends and any capital gains distributions in additional shares.
**Partial Year—Explorer II began operations on June 7, 1985; Vanguard Specialized Portfolios began operations on May 23, 1984; Windsor II began operations on June 24, 1985; Vanguard STAR Fund began operations on March 28, 1985; Vanguard Insured Long-Term Portfolio began operations on September 30, 1984.

· SEVEN ·

The Big Game Hunt: Buying Individual Stocks That Soar

I think mutual funds are the best way for most people to invest in the stock market. Properly selected, equity funds provide the diversification you need to protect your assets. The better portfolio managers have training and expertise most investors cannot hope to match. And with more than a thousand mutual funds now on the market, choosing the right funds can be as challenging and as much fun as picking the right stocks.

That's my opinion. But I also realize that for many investors, funds do not satisfy their emotional needs. They must have direct ownership in specific companies. Being able to say "I own part of Consolidated Widgets" brings them a satisfaction they'll never get from ownership of Consolidated Fund shares.

I understand and sympathize with this emotional need, and if you fit that description this chapter is for you. I'll show you some sensible ways to decide which stocks to buy—guidelines you can use in ever-changing circumstances. It is also true that as you become more experienced in your investments, and have more to invest, it makes more and more sense to devote a portion of your assets to individually selected stocks. So whether you plan to buy stocks now or in the future, read on.

First, I will show you how to select what I call "foundation stocks." You must have your basic stock portfolio in mutual funds or these foundation stocks. If not, you're not investing; you're speculating, with all the risk that implies. Once we've covered these basics, I will show you how to use additional funds to go for the big kills with more speculative stocks—what I call "the big game hunt."

Foundation Portfolios

When you build a house, you start with the foundation. You insist on a solid bedrock foundation to keep your house from sliding down the slope or sinking in the mud when the first bad weather hits.

Your stock portfolio must be built with the same fundamental care. Use solid foundation stocks to build your nest egg, to save for retirement or the children's education, or to manage IRA, pension, and profit-sharing programs. Forget the speculative stocks until you have finished with this foundation.

To start, let me give you five ground rules to follow:

1. Do not be a trader.

2. Buy for the long term.

3. Do not buy new issues or secondary offerings.

4. Do not be sold stocks. Do your own research and make your own decisions. With my guidelines you can do as good a job as any salesperson and usually a much better job.

5. Buy your stock selections through a discount broker. You will be treated professionally, and you will save commission dollars.

Now, the very essence of a portfolio is *diversification.* A handful of stocks, or stocks all in one or two industries, must be considered a speculation no matter which stocks you hold. A number of objective statistical studies have shown that a portfolio of thirty-five stocks (in different fields or industries, of course) gives you virtually the same diversification as owning all the stocks on the New York Stock Exchange. But even fifteen or twenty selections are not necessary or advisable until you have a portfolio of substantial value. A minimum of ten stock positions in different industries will give you more than 80 percent of the diversification you'd have from the entire membership of the New York Stock Exchange.

Let's plan, then, to start by assembling a portfolio of ten stocks in different industries. Once you do this, it will be necessary to sell one of your holdings whenever you wish to add a new name to your portfolio. This requires *discipline.* Discipline is a cornerstone word in my investment vocabulary. You must be disciplined, unemotional, and patient in your selections.

Now, what kind of stocks should you buy? Here is a basic list of things to look for, in no particular order of importance.

Be a buyer of value. How do you judge value? One way is to look at the price of a given stock in relation to book value per share. Avoid stocks with a book value below the price per share.

Look for low price/earnings ratios. This is such an important and proven strategy that I will devote some discussion to this shortly.

Buy only stocks that pay a dividend and that have not had a dividend cut in the past ten years. I am suspicious of companies that cut dividends. I have no set rule as to how high dividends should be, but I do like a dividend of at least 4 percent.

Look for a solid record of earnings. Do not buy companies that are losing money. Dynamic growth is not vital, but modest growth is necessary.

Seek easy-to-understand companies. If you cannot comprehend the company's product line, the stock doesn't belong in your foundation portfolio.

Look for established but smaller to medium-sized companies that are out of favor or too small for the big institutional players.

I like companies with no debt. If the company has debt, it should be quite modest in relation to the equity value of the company. Compare the company's debt growth over the past five years to its book value or dividends. If debt is growing faster than book value or dividends, forget the company.

Dull-looking companies often make the best vehicles for a foundation stock portfolio. Such companies can frequently be the target of takeovers and leveraged buyouts.

I prefer low-priced stocks, but that is not one of my hard and fast rules.

Do your research with these guidelines in mind, then buy during a recession (see Chapter 9) and nurture your portfolio with patience and discipline.

In Search of Low Price/Earnings Ratios: David Dreman's Strategy

The price/earnings (P/E) ratio is the price of a stock divided by its earnings per share. For example, a stock now selling for $20 a share that earned $2 per share last year has a P/E ratio of 10. If it had earnings of $4 per share, its P/E ratio would be 5.

The P/E ratio gives investors an idea of how much they are paying for the company's earning power. To understand this clearly, let's assume two companies with earnings of $10 per share. One stock sells for $50 per share (its P/E ratio, therefore, is 5) while the other sells for $100 per share (giving it a P/E ratio of 10). Other things being equal, I'd buy the stock selling for $50—the one with the low P/E ratio. You are getting more for your money. In this instance, for $100 you can buy *two* shares and earn $20 with the low P/E company—twice as much as with the high P/E stock.

Now, what is a "low" P/E? In theory, below 10—that is, the stock price will be less than 10 times the earnings. At the same time I avoid stocks with *very* low P/E ratios—say, 1, 2, or 3. A P/E ratio that low often implies some kind of problem that requires the company to pay exorbitant dividends in order to keep the stock from sinking. On the other hand, a low P/E ratio can reflect a temporary situation, such as a one-time sale of valuable real estate or other assets.

A glance at the stock tables in the *Wall Street Journal* or your local newspaper will also show stocks with P/E ratios higher than 20—perhaps 25, 30, or more. These are usually young, fast-growing companies that often pay no dividends at all. They may have a place in your "big game hunt" portfolio, but they don't belong here, in your foundation portfolio.

You want stocks with a low P/E ratio *and* a record of consistent dividend payments. For this foundation portfolio, therefore, we will avoid the riskier stocks with P/E ratios higher than 10. Our best bets are stocks with P/E ratios of 7 to 10. To help you discover these stocks, the Value Line Investment Survey, *Forbes* magazine, and other information sources frequently run screens identifying low P/E stocks.

The low P/E investment strategy was popularized by David Dreman, a *Forbes* magazine columnist and author of *The New*

Contrarian Investment Strategy. This is one of the most valuable books you can read for advice on stock selection, and in it Dreman gives the statistical evidence that low P/E stocks outperform high P/E stocks.

Brokerage Stocks: A Special Opportunity

Publicly traded brokerage house shares offer especially good opportunities for investors during the early stages of a bull market. Because their "industry" is the stock market itself, they tend to exaggerate the movements of the stock market. When they're bad, they are very bad; when they're good, they are very good indeed.

In my investment pantheon, brokerage stocks have a special niche somewhere between my foundation portfolio and my "big game hunt" of speculative stocks. As I've noted, brokerage stocks tend to swing more wildly than most foundation stocks. At the same time, though, they are not speculations and many of them have to be considered blue-chip issues. I'd suggest you include one brokerage stock in a ten-stock foundation portfolio; it can represent the financial industry. If you have a foundation portfolio of fifteen to twenty stocks, you could include two brokerage stocks.

David Dreman shares my enthusiasm for brokerage stocks, and he explained why in an interview in *Innovators,* one of my publications.

"Brokerage firms make the same mistake over and over again," Dreman says. "During the exciting, early stages of the bull market cycle, they build excess capacity which eventually collides with moderating revenues. Margins are squeezed, and earnings head south [go down]. The brokerage houses are repeatedly guilty of building mausoleums at the first stage market peaks.

"Ironically," Dreman continues, "investors share in the industry's penchant for repeating the same mistake. They can't get enough of the brokerage stocks near market peaks and wouldn't think of buying them near the bottoms. This is precisely the kind of investor overreaction the low P/E strategy is designed to take advantage of."

As with other types of stocks, the best time to buy is in the midst of a recession. You will be buying at bargain-basement prices and poised for the next bull market explosion. Following are three brokerage stocks to track and consider buying in the next recession.

Discount Corporation of New York

("DCNY" over-the-counter) 58 Pine Street, New York, NY 10005. Telephones (212) 248-8989 and (212) 248-8900.

DCNY is not a household name. It is not a retail operation like the next two brokerage houses. It is, however, a certified blue chip within the closed confines of the discreet institutional brokerage business.

DCNY is one of a small handful of primary dealers in federal securities. It makes markets in U.S. Treasury bills, notes, and bonds as well as obligations of federally sponsored agencies such as the Federal National Mortgage Association, the Federal Home Loan Bank, and the Federal Farm Credit Bank. DCNY also makes markets in negotiable certificates of deposit, bankers' acceptances, and bank holding companies' commercial paper. And it deals in repurchase agreements and trades foreign exchange for its customers.

Publicity is shunned at DCNY. The company's wafer-thin annual report offers only the basics; no four-color layouts and glowing summaries of past success. The management is both austere and very, very private. Among DCNY's directors are former Federal Reserve Board member Scott E. Pardee, Exxon senior vice president Jack F. Bennett, former Chase Manhattan chairman George Champion, and John J. Scanlon, former executive vice-president at AT&T.

You get the picture. This is a very sophisticated, small, and well-managed outfit. One gets the feeling that if these distinguished men can't get it right, then no one can.

Legg Mason, Inc.

("LM" on the NYSE) 7 East Redwood Street, Baltimore, MD 21202. Telephones (800) 822-5544 and (301) 539-3400.

Legg Mason is a major regional investment brokerage firm that concentrates on individual rather than institutional investors. Most of these clients are located in Maryland, the District of Columbia, Pennsylvania, and Virginia.

Legg Mason also emphasizes value analyses in making its stock selections. In other words, it follows the type of analysis I outlined earlier in this chapter—it seeks companies that represent quality, with a good record of paying dividends, and low P/E ratios. Its record in picking these companies has been outstanding, leading to the formation of a stock mutual fund, Legg Mason Value Trust. The firm also has two money market funds—Legg Mason Cash Reserve Trust and Legg Mason Tax Exempt Trust.

In addition to these funds and the retail brokerage operation, Legg Mason acts as an underwriter as well as a financial advisor to municipalities, school districts, and other specialized government units. Putting this all together, annual revenues have increased over the past five years from $31 million to more than $70 million.

In an industry cluttered with boiler-room mentality and sweatshop tactics, Legg Mason stands out for its integrity and ability to put its customers' interests first. Perhaps this is why the company's book value has quadrupled in just the last four years. I have confidence in the future of this quality investment organization.

A. G. Edwards, Inc.

("AGE" on the NYSE) One North Jefferson, St. Louis, MO 63103. Telephones (800) 551-2644 and (314) 289-3000.

This financial services company is noted for its efficiency and strong client loyalty, both rarities in the retail brokerage industry. Nearly a hundred years old, it is a premium regional investment firm that has expanded to over 260 offices in forty-two states.

I have followed the company's fortunes for many years and think well of its management. I believe that Chairman and President Benjamin F. Edwards III is a strong and capable chief executive officer. Under his leadership the firm has avoided the problem areas that have crippled less astutely managed investment organizations.

Since 1981 revenues have expanded from $186 million to over $300 million annually. Over the same period, book value has climbed from $6.87 per share to $13.97 per share—more than double in only four years. Management's ability to earn between 15 and 30 percent consistently has allowed A. G. Edwards, Inc., to raise its dividend three times in the last four years.

And Now, the Big Game Hunt Begins . . .

Every investor seeks to catch the big one—the big winner, the stock that doubles and then doubles again. You can participate in this big game hunt, though it's not as easy as building your portfolio of foundation stocks.

Above all: big game hunting portfolios must use only risk capital! First you must get your foundation portfolio in order. Do not place your retirement or education funds in this big game hunting portfolio. If you can afford to take some substantial risks in a quest for big profits, big game hunting is for you. To give yourself the best chance at coming out ahead in this speculative area, follow my four basic guidelines:

1. Above all, buy for long-term capital gains. Do not be a trader.

2. Seek companies that are at the cutting edge of new technologies and concepts. I monitor companies on the leading edge of the semiconductor industry, health science companies including genetic engineering firms, and consumer electronics companies.

3. As with foundation stocks, follow the portfolio approach, to spread and minimize risk. Build a portfolio of at least ten positions. If your excess funds are substantial, I would move up to twenty positions.

4. Buy during a recession. The types of stocks I am going to list for you will no doubt decline sharply in price before and during the early stages of the next recession. Wait until the carnage unfolds and then pick over the stock market rubble to build your distress-sale portfolio.

First I am going to give you eight guidelines to use in investing in high-tech opportunities. Then I will briefly describe three emerging medical technologies that are especially promising. Then I will give you six companies to track. These companies appear to be good candidates for my big game hunting portfolio. I will continue to follow the progress of each, however, to decide whether they should be on my master list when the next recession takes its toll on the stock market. You should do that too.

Eight Guidelines for High-Tech Investing

In 1976 Key Pharmaceuticals was a small, $3 million sales company researching innovative drug delivery systems. Key stock sold at $4 per share. By 1980 Key Pharmaceuticals had sales of $23 million and a stock price of $36 per share, due to a single product, Theo-Dur, a sustained-release drug for treating bronchial asthma. Adjusted for stock splits, a $4,000 investment had turned into $230,000 in just four years.

In 1981 Biochem looked like a "sure thing" medical technology company. Biochem had patents on sophisticated electronic instruments capable of instantaneously measuring blood gases and blood pressure, vital processes in anesthesiology. Biochem was selling its products and making money. By the spring of 1983, the stock was trading at 17⅝. Within a year it was down to 4, however, and the company was filing for Chapter 11 bankruptcy.

I use these two examples to illustrate the *enormous opportunity and great risk* inherent in high-technology stock investing. Fortunes will be made in high-tech stocks in the years ahead, and fortunes will also be lost. I believe in high technology and in taking advantage of the investment opportunities it will continue to present in the future. However, I am also a prudent investor. I believe that assessing potential risk is every bit as important as evaluating prospective rewards. These eight guidelines should help you to profit rather than perish in the high technology stock market.

1. The Technology

The first step in evaluating a high-technology company is to try to assess just how unique and special its products really are. Technology companies do not operate in a vacuum. Despite promoters' claims, there are relatively few companies with totally proprietary technology. A given company may be farther along in research and development, or it may be able to manufacture a high-tech product more economically, but it usually does not have the whole field to itself.

A perfect example is the computer "floppy disk" business, which several years ago was thought to be the exclusive province of just one small company. The company was a Wall Street darling, trading at an astronomical multiple to earnings, when out of nowhere a half dozen companies emerged with comparable floppy disk technology. The stock sank like a rock, taking many an unwary stockholder down with it. As Hartwell Growth Fund's founder, John Hartwell, put it, "floppy disk technology proved about as proprietary as popcorn."

2. The Market

Equity Research Associates' John Westergaard, a pioneer of high-tech oriented growth stock investing, is fond of pointing out that technology, in and of itself, does not necessarily make a prosperous high-technology company or a good investment. The ability to spin straw into gold is only as valuable as the gold itself.

In short, technology will not be profitable unless there is a market for it. Westergaard cautions investors to focus on the potential market rather than on the wondrous nature of the technology itself. Xerox, one of Westergaard's earliest discoveries, did not evolve from a struggling young company into a Fortune 500 giant just because it perfected the photocopying process. It became a household name because there was a market for this technology.

3. Selling Technology

If truly proprietary technology is the first ingredient in the recipe for the ideal high-tech company, and a ready market is the second, then the third and no less essential element is management that knows how to reach its market.

The Nova Fund's Bruce Everitt, one of the investment industry's pre-eminent high-technology analysts, spends as much or more time talking with a high-tech company's marketing executive as he does with its research and development chief. The reason? High-tech companies and their shareholders make money when products are sold, not when they are created. Everitt points out that in numerous instances small companies with technologically superior products fail, while competitors that are steps behind technologically succeed simply because of their more effective marketing organizations.

Everitt recommends that amateur high-tech analysts visit technology retailers. For example, if you think there's money to be made in computer software stocks, a chat with the sales clerk at Businessland about what's moving off the shelves may be more valuable than a technical critique of competing software packages.

4. Timing: Is the Future Now, Yesterday, or Years Away?

In the high-technology stock market, the early bird catches the worm. To profit from high-tech investment opportunities, you must spot them ahead of the crowd. By the time a high-tech stock is the subject of cocktail party conversation, it is usually past its prime as a potentially profitable investment idea. Perhaps the most common error in high-tech investing is to buy a stock after it's already doubled or tripled, thinking it is bound to do so again. No tree grows to the sky.

At the same time, being too early can cost you money. A good example is the genetic engineering stocks. The technology and its future promise are terribly exciting. However, several years ago when investors first discovered genetic engineering, biotech companies were years away from developing marketable products. Yet, new issues were being snapped up at unbelievable prices.

Since then, many of these stocks have fallen 50, 75, or even 100 percent despite the great strides being made in research and development. Today, the better genetic engineering firms are introducing products and starting to make money, but most investors don't seem to be interested in their stocks. Those that are may be poised to make a lot of money.

5. Competition

Competition is the bane of young high-technology companies and their shareholders. Human nature and economics dictate that whenever someone discovers a good thing, everyone wants to get in on it. Patents and technological innovations offer some protection from competition. However, slightly different technologies are often aimed at the same markets, thereby making patent protection virtually worthless. Patents also eventually expire, paving the way for intense competition, often from bigger, more financially powerful companies.

Alfred Ondis, chairman of Astro-Med, a highly successful producer of technologically sophisticated graphic recorders and printers, has an excellent strategy for protecting his company and its shareholders from future competition from larger high-tech companies. He develops products for relatively small "niche" markets that, despite rapid growth, are not yet large enough to attract the attention of the big boys. Ondis points out that by targeting these niche markets while they are small, and growing with them, he has a big head start over potential competitors.

Many investment professionals follow this strategy also. Rich Fentin, manager of Fidelity Mercury Fund, and Frank Wisneski, the man behind Vanguard's Explorer Fund, credit much of their success to investing in high-tech companies that exploit fast-growing niche markets.

6. Diversify

Noted medical technology analyst George Stasen, currently running the closed-end Emerging Medical Technology Fund, often points out that investing in high-technology stocks demands humility. With so many uncertainties to contend with, even the most knowledgeable, experienced high-tech investor is going to make his or her share of mistakes. To avoid getting clobbered by these inevitable mistakes, Stasen and many others use a diversified approach to high-tech investing. For example, if Stasen feels that genetic engineering is an area of great investment opportunity, he will invest in a half dozen or more genetic engineering stocks. Stasen concedes that perhaps only 60 percent of his choices will prosper. However, he feels that the winners will more than compensate for the losers.

Individual investors cannot afford to diversify as extensively as can a professional managing large sums of money, but putting all your eggs in one basket is not the way to win at the high-technology stock game. It is better to buy fewer shares of two or three companies in a promising high-tech industry than to place one big bet on a potential winner.

7. Look at the Balance Sheet

The best technology, like the best business idea in any industry, is valueless unless you have the financial resources to implement it. Any small business consultant will tell you that the number one reason for the overwhelming majority of small business failures is insufficient capital. This is particularly true of high-technology companies that need large sums of money for research and development to support growth and, most importantly, to survive the cost-cutting wars resulting from intense competition.

The smart high-tech investor takes a careful look at the balance sheet. I do not have space here to offer a full lesson on balance sheet analysis, but you should be wary of high-technology companies with excessive debt-to-equity and weak net working capital positions.

8. Watch the Investment Market

While some investors manage to make money in any kind of market, it is much easier if you are running with the bulls. When the market in general, and high-technology stocks in particular, are bearish, you are not likely to make a killing regardless of how well a company is doing.

This does not mean that you should be buying high-tech stocks when it looks as if nothing can go wrong and everyone is talking about their big winners. In fact, this is precisely the time you should be most wary. I have found the new issues market to be a good barometer for high-tech investors to watch. When it is hot and everything with a high-tech name is being sold out, buyers should beware. When you cannot give away a high-technology new issue, smart investors are getting ready to buy.

Three Emerging Medical Technology Fields to Watch

Laser Surgery

Laser technology is almost a quarter-century old, yet many creative uses for lasers are just now being developed. One of the most promising applications is in the field of surgery. Scientists feel that in the not too distant future, the laser will replace the scalpel as the primary surgical tool. Laser instruments are precise, cause less trauma to tissue, result in less bleeding, and can be used in virtually every type of surgical operation.

Argon lasers are already being used extensively in eye surgery. The development of the CO_2 laser for gynecologic, orthopedic, and dermatologic procedures and the Nd-YAG laser for brain, gastrointestinal, and cancer surgery, promises to expand vastly the use of lasers in America's operating rooms.

A recent research report from the brokerage firm of Swergold, Chefitz and Sinasbaugh, Inc., estimates that the U.S. medical laser market will grow from its current $75 million to $500 million by 1990 and $1 billion by the turn of the century. With this kind of projected growth, laser technology companies very probably deserve some investment attention.

As is often the case with emerging high-technology, many young companies are in the forefront. Following is a list of publicly traded companies in the medical laser field. I suggest you write them for an annual report, or ask your personal investment advisor to do some research for you. Do not forget to apply the guidelines I have provided in evaluating these investment ideas.

1. Coherent, Inc. ("COHR" over-the-counter), 3210 Porter Drive, Palo Alto, CA 94304.

2. Endo-Tase, Inc. ("ENDL" over-the-counter), 10 Columbus Avenue, Ste. 2195, New York, NY 10019.

3. Lasermed Corp. ("LAMD" over-the-counter), 151 Kalmus, Ste. H-3, Costa Mesa, CA 92626.

4. Laser Corp. ("LSER" over-the-counter), 1832 South 3850 West, Salt Lake City, UT 84104.

5. Laser Photonics ("LAZR" over-the-counter), 2025 Palmridge Way, Orlando, FL 32809.

6. Lasers for Medicine ("LFMI" over-the-counter), 80 Davids Drive, Hauppauge, NY 11788.

Monoclonal Antibodies: Cancer Scouts

Cancer research has produced relatively effective weapons for killing cancerous cells. Radiation and anticancer drugs do the job. Unfortunately, they don't do it selectively. In the process of attacking cancer cells, healthy tissue is also destroyed. This limits dosages and therefore total effectiveness. Also, side effects are often as painful and distressing as the disease itself. One of the great challenges in current cancer research is to develop selective delivery systems for proven cancer killers.

Monoclonal antibodies may be the key. Monoclonal antibodies are genetically engineered duplicates of natural human antibodies. Like natural antibodies, monoclonals are coded to attack infected cells and bypass healthy ones. Biotechnologists are experimenting with using monoclonals to deliver cancer killers directly and specifically to infected cells, thereby limiting or possibly even eliminating damage to healthy tissue. Large tumors would still require surgical removal. However, postsurgical injections of monoclonals bonded to anticancer agents would mop up any cancerous cells the scalpel may have missed.

Monoclonal antibodies are already being used successfully in new diagnostic procedures for a range of diseases including herpes. Researchers expect monoclonals to be used soon in treatments for some infections. The effective use of monoclonals in cancer treatment may still be years away. However, the company or companies that perfect a monoclonal treatment for today's most dreaded killer will enrich medical science and themselves.

As one would expect, the potential for monoclonal-based cancer treatment has attracted many players, including most of the large ethical drug companies. Some of the most promising developments, however, are coming from a handful of smaller, publicly held biotechnology firms. Two of the more prominent ones are listed below, and readers who are interested in exploring their investment potential should write for an annual report or ask their broker for information on the firms.

1. Centacor, Inc., 244 Great Valley Parkway, Malvern, PA 19355.

2. Cetus Corp., 1400 53rd Street, Emeryville, CA 94608.

Electronic Painkillers

Many people live with persistent pain caused by arthritis, spinal disorders, or irreparable nerve damage. While effective cures for these specific ailments may be years away, medical scientists have perfected new techniques for alleviating chronic pain. The most advanced of these techniques is TENS, an acronym for transcutaneous electrical nerve stimulation.

TENS systems eliminate persistent pain by blocking the pain signal sent by the nerves to the brain. These systems can be operated via electrodes taped to the skin or implanted in the human body. The electrodes are activated by a pulse generator. Patients report that periodic TENS treatments eventually provide relief from chronic pain.

Medical Technology Fund's Jennifer Byrne reports that Medtronic (6970 Central Avenue, Minneapolis, MN 55432) now has a variety of TENS-oriented equipment on the market. The company's Pisces and SE-4 systems are basic electronic painkillers. The Federal Drug Administration's Neurological Devices Panel has also recommended Medtronics's Itrel, a TENS system implanted in the spinal column. The company also manufactures MultiFlex, an electronic nerve stimulation system for treating accident, stroke, and spinal disease victims.

Other publicly held companies making TENS equipment include Mentor Corp. (2700 Freeway Boulevard, Minneapolis, MN 55430) and Staodynamics (1225 Florida Avenue, Longmont, CO 80501). Readers who suffer from chronic pain should certainly ask their doctors for information on the new electronic painkillers. Investors who want to learn more about this exciting new medical technology should write the firms mentioned or ask their broker for more information.

Six "Big Game" High-Tech Companies to Track and Hunt in Recession

Finally, let's look at six candidates for your big game hunt portfolio. I will give you brief thumbnail sketches of these companies. I will be tracking them closely for "portfolio candidacy" during the next recession. If you are ready for the big game hunt, you should follow their tracks too.

Chiron Corporation

("CHIR" over-the-counter) 4560 Horton Street, Emeryville, CA 94608.

Chiron is a young company in the exploding field of genetic engineering. It is named after the mythical centaur Chiron (ki-ron), who was renowned for skill in medicine and the healing arts. This modern-day Chiron is a biotechnology company focusing on vaccines, therapeutic hormones, enzymes, and diagnostics.

Since its inception, Chiron has focused on research and brought in quality marketing partners to put its products into the field. As a result, high-quality royalties income is an important factor in the company's long-term growth program. Chiron's technological expertise is well recognized, as demonstrated by the fact that three of the five largest pharmaceutical companies in the world are project partners with Chiron. Its hepatitis B vaccine is being brought to market by Merck & Co., Inc., without question the best marketer of state-of-the-art vaccines in the world.

Chiron is now making the transition from a company with primary focus on research to a broader-based company with significant attention to product development and biological manufacturing. Already a leader, it has shown a distinct ability to innovate and attract high-powered international recognition and support.

Symbolics, Inc.

("SMBX" over-the-counter) 11 Cambridge Center, Cambridge, MA 02142.

Symbolics, Inc., is the world leader in the development, manufacturing, and marketing of advanced computer systems that facilitate the use of artificial intelligence and other related Symbolics processing techniques. The company was founded by a group of scientists from the Massachusetts Institute of Technology.

Symbolics computers incorporate enormous memories and an integrated software environment consisting of many software tools. Among the targets of Symbolics computers is the market for hazardous tasks—areas generally requiring human judgment, such as the management of a nuclear power plant or the loading of liquid fuel for the space shuttle.

A wide array of companies are already using Symbolics computers and Symbolics processing techniques to automate the industrial process. Alcoa, the world's leading producer of aluminum products, is working to automate its aluminum manufacturing process still further, and is succeeding by using Symbolics processing techniques. The Symbolics 3600 family of computers is playing a key role in Alcoa's process.

NASA has undertaken major projects designed to automate a vast array of tasks involved in the space shuttle program. NASA has at least eight separate expert systems projects underway at the Johnson and Kennedy space centers. Symbolics equipment is being used as a foundation in the development and implementation of these systems.

The Economist put it well in its August 10, 1985, issue. In a special science and technology feature headed "Japan's Soft Point," *The Economist* wrote: "American software writers would not be caught dead without their ($100,000 plus) Symbolics work stations; too many Japanese make do with pencil and paper."

Symbolics, Inc., the major force in the development of the commercial marketplace for symbolic processing, is uniquely positioned to aid America in improving productivity in the 1980s and 1990s.

Genentech, Inc.

("GENE" over-the-counter) 460 Point San Bruno Boulevard, South San Francisco, CA 94080.

Many scientists believe that recombinant DNA will be a powerful factor in overcoming today's leading causes of death. Genentech, Inc., is at the forefront of recombinant DNA technology.

Exciting new Genentech products are in the pipeline. These include tissue-type plasminogen activator to treat heart attacks, and gamma interferon and tumor necrosis factor to fight cancer. Genentech's human insulin product to treat diabetes is already on the market.

Cancer is the number two killer in the United States (after heart attacks). Genentech scientists point out that cancer is not a single disease but rather well over a hundred diseases, so it is unlikely that any one drug will cure cancer. In the fight against cancer Genentech is developing a family of proteins.

In just the last few years, more than a score of oncogenes— genes that cause cancer—have been identified. Oncogenes are basically altered versions of ordinary benign genes present in healthy cells. Like most genes, they direct the production of proteins. Normal cells are turned into cancer cells when proteins encoded by oncogenes function abnormally. Genentech is at the forefront of research into the oncogene function through its expertise in recombinant DNA technology.

Cray Research, Inc.

("CYR" on the NYSE) 608 Second Avenue South, Minneapolis, MN 55402.

Led by the genius, Seymour Cray, Cray Research is the worldwide leader in supercomputers. To date, Cray has provided nearly 70 percent of supercomputers operating worldwide. A single Cray system sells for almost $18 million.

Cray's recently introduced supercomputer, Cray-2, is the fastest in the world. The very first Cray-2 system is now working in fusion energy calculations for the Lawrence Livermore National Laboratory in Livermore, California. The Cray-2 contains 240,000 computer chips, can send and receive data simultaneously on as many as thirty-six disk drives, and makes over one billion calculations a second. It sports the largest central memory (over two billion bytes) and fastest clock cycle time (4.1 billionths of a second) of any commercial system.

Cray, the world leader in state-of-the-art supercomputers, will continue to break into new frontiers for physical simulation through analysis of the behavior of physical systems.

LSI Logic Corporation

("LLSI" over-the-counter) 1551 McCarthy Boulevard, Milpitas, CA 95035.

LSI is the acknowledged leader in application-specific integrated circuits (ASICs). In fact, the ASIC business is LSI's only business. And what are ASICs? They are semiconductors customized to the unique needs of LSI customers, such as General Motors Corporation. ASICs are the building blocks of a wide array of products, ranging from satellites and reference systems to computers and telephones. The ASIC sector of the semiconductor market is the single fastest growing segment of the entire semiconductor industry.

LSI is unique in that it manufactures, assembles, packages, and tests virtually all its circuits in the United States. Quality control is ensured. New products such as structured arrays and structured cells will keep LSI in the forefront of the rapidly expanding ASIC market of the 1980s.

Biogen

("BGENF" over-the-counter) 14 Cambridge Center, Cambridge, MA 02142.

Biogen is a forerunner in the development of pharmaceutical products through genetic engineering. Through the process of recombinant DNA, Biogen scientists can unravel a cell's DNA molecule, the blueprint for all living matter. Biogen scientists are now able to reconstruct life's basic elements to provide products of immense long-term benefit to society. For example, the company is developing human proteins for the treatment and prevention of stroke, heart attack, and cancer.

Biogen's master plan centers on the commercialization of genetic engineering. Biogen is the only company that has begun testing both interleukin-2 and gamma interferon on humans, and it was also the first company to begin recombinant gamma interferon human clinical trials. In 1984 the company began construction of a production plant in Switzerland, and it is hoped that by the time the plant is completed Biogen will be able to introduce gamma interferon on a commercial basis.

There are few companies in the world that can match Biogen for scientific expertise in genetic engineering.

Over the long term, the majority of my assets will always be placed in value-oriented foundation stocks or funds. Once every few years, however, I am willing to go on a big game hunt such as the one I've outlined here. If you plan to use *excess* speculative funds, and are ready to take the risk, you may also reap outstanding rewards. Happy hunting!

· EIGHT ·

Stock Options: The Financial Armadillo's Lottery Ticket

Would you like to make a 5,000 percent profit on your investment within four months?

Yes? I thought so. That's why this section on "digging for profits" would not be complete without a few words on stock options. I call stock options the Financial Armadillo's "lottery ticket," because when you win, you're likely to win really big, and when you lose, you only lose the price of your ticket—your option.

That sounds like a pretty good deal so far. Now comes the bad news, of course. And the bad news is that you're much more likely to lose than win.

When you buy a state's lottery ticket—the kind we're all familiar with—you realize that the odds of winning the jackpot are miniscule. You buy the ticket anyway because it's a cheap way to dream of sudden riches and what you would do if that were *your* picture in the newspapers. Yet there are people who see this as more than a game. They become addicted to the idea of winning, and go broke buying those dollar tickets.

The stock options lottery is also a gamble—"speculation" is the word used in polite financial circles—but it's not as random as a lottery. If you follow some basic guidelines, such as the ones I'll give you in this chapter, you stand a much better chance of winning something here than you do in the lottery. But then your ticket costs much more, too. Instead of $1 or $2, it is likely to set you back $300, $500, or $800. You can see that it doesn't take too many losing tickets in the stock options lottery to make the performance record of your investment portfolio look very dismal indeed.

Therefore, two hard-and-fast rules *must* be observed by any Financial Armadillo who wants to play in this lottery:

Rule No. 1: Don't put any money down until you have some experience in more traditional investments—at the very least, a full business cycle of investing. Get a feel for the market, and what happens to stocks during all phases of the business cycle, before you move into stock options in even the most limited way.

While you're waiting, it might be a good idea to construct an imaginary portfolio of stock options. Make your selections on paper, note the amount of money you've "invested," and keep track of what happens to those options. This might be such a sobering experience that you won't have any need for Rule No. 2.

Rule No. 2: Never put your bread money into options. And when I say never, I mean *never,* no matter how experienced you have become. Experienced options players have made millions over a couple of months, only to see that fortune wiped out the following week. Any money you place on options should be excess "play" or "speculation" money you still have after taking care of the Financial Armadillo's portfolio of Treasury securities, gold, mutual funds, and such. In fact, I'll show you one way to devise a system where you won't have to feel guilty even if every one of your stock options lottery tickets is a loser.

A No-Lose Strategy

Place 90 percent of your money in the "risk-free" investment, ninety-day Treasury bills. The remaining 10 percent will be your "play" money for speculating in stock options. Every six months you add up the money in both piles and again divide it so that 90 percent is in Treasury bills and the remainder in options.

For example, let's make the math easy and say you started with $100,000. Of that, $90,000 is in T-bills earning interest and $10,000 is in options. Let's say you do pretty well, and at the end of six months your $10,000 has grown to $20,000. Meanwhile, your T-bills have earned $4,000 in interest. You now have $94,000 from T-bills and $20,000 from options, for a total of $114,000. You place 90 percent of this, or $102,000, in T-bills and Treasury funds. That leaves you $12,000 this time around to invest in options.

Since you are not likely to lose *all* the money you committed to options, this should continue for some time and give you experience in improving your options performance. The really great advantage is that you can give yourself this education— and hope for the "big kill" in options—knowing that at least 90 percent of your money is safe.

Even if you make that big kill in options, you should continue with this strategy. Remember that one reversal in the stock market could wipe out 90 percent of even a widely diversified options portfolio. By following this strategy, you use your winning options "lottery ticket" to build your total portfolio, and you never have more than 10 percent of your money at speculative risk.

What Are Options?

Basically, options are a way to bet on the future direction of an individual stock, a financial instrument, or the stock market in general. For explanatory purposes, I'll use a simple stock option—an option to one particular stock.

A *call option* is a contract that gives you the right (the option) to buy a hundred shares of that stock at a specific, predetermined price during a specific period of time. A *put option* is the opposite. It gives you the right (the option) to sell a hundred shares of that stock for a specified price within a certain period. You may have heard the term, "puts and calls." This is what that term refers to.

For every options contract there has to be a buyer and a seller, of course. As with the stock itself, this is handled anonymously by the stock exchanges. The price of the option contract is called its *premium,* and that price is determined by supply and demand. The buyer pays the premium to the seller.

As a general rule, most sellers are wealthy individuals or institutions with vast stock holdings, and they sell options to increase the earnings of their stock portfolio. And as a general rule most buyers of options are smaller, individual investors. Therefore, I'll be illustrating this discussion with examples of call options from here on out.

Let's look at two of the factors in your call option—price and time.

I said that a call option gives you the right to buy one hundred shares of the stock at a specific, predetermined price. The price you select is called the *strike price,* or *exercise price.* The strike price can be above the current price of the stock, near the present price, or below its present price. If, for example, a stock is now priced at $43, you will probably find options listed for $30, $35, $40, $45, $50, and $55.

As for time, options mature every three months. At any point in time, options will be available for no more than the next three expirations. The longest term for any option, therefore, is nine months. For example, the stock that interests you may have options expiring in March, June, September, and December. If it is now January, you will have a choice of March, June, and September options.

Options are a fascinating world, and the strategies you can use range from wild to conservative—yes, there are sophisticated conservative strategies you can use to hedge against losses in your stock portfolio. To learn about all these possibilities, read the free booklets available from the Chicago Board Options Exchange (Room 2200, LaSalle at Jackson, Chicago, IL 60604, telephone (800) 332-2263 or (312) 786-5600). Especially read Max G. Ansbacher's *The New Options Market* (New York: Walker, 1975). He makes options more understandable than anyone I know.

Right now we're concerned about digging for profits, and specifically about making big money fast. Let's see how we can try to do this.

How (Hopefully) to Make Big Money
Fast in Options

The enticing thing about a call option is the way it limits the amount of capital you have to put up, while it increases your potential reward. To illustrate, let's say you foresee a bull market or continuing bull market, and you expect XYZ stock in particular to rise dramatically.

XYZ stock presently sells for $80 per share. For $2 per share you buy an option that gives you the right to buy the stock for $90 per share within the next two months. Since each contract is for 100 shares, you have to put up $200 as your premium. That's much better, you note, than having to put up $8,000 for 100 shares of the stock.

Now, this stock will have to rise above $90 per share before you make a profit. We want a happy ending, so let's say the stock rises to $95 before the expiration of your option. The option you bought for $2 is now worth $5, since it allows you to buy the stock at a $5 discount (you're buying a $95 stock for $90). Note that the stock's price has increased by 18.75 percent ($80 to $95), but the option's price has increased 250 percent (from $2 to $5). You have decreased the amount of your capital at risk and increased your percentage of profit dramatically.

Note also that you don't buy or sell the stock itself, just the option on the stock. When the stock rises to $95 you sell the option for $5. The person who bought that option from you, through a broker, obviously thinks the stock and the option are going to continue going up, while you are willing to take your profits.

At this point you may remember the opening of this chapter. "A 250 percent return in two months is fine," you say, "especially compared with an annual return of 25 percent from my growth stock fund and 10 percent from my Treasury note. But Dick, where's that 5,000-percent profit you promised me?"

Well, when the price of Boeing stock went from 29⅞ to 72⅛, the premium of the 35 option went from 11/16 to 37. And when Bally Manufacturing stock went from 16 to 65½ within a few months, the 20 option went from ⅞ to 48. Both of those options increased by around 5,300 percent. In other words, for each $1,000 spent on either of those options, you could have earned $53,000 within a few months.

Obviously this is not a regular, normal event, or I'd be spending all my time buying options for myself rather than advising you. Those two examples are extraordinary in themselves, and they assume that you bought and sold at just the right time for maximum profits. In real life, we usually settle for something less, rather than risk losing everything. But these examples do show you the potential in stock options, and I suspect they will give you some inspiration as well.

What gives you the greatest *potential* for such a spectacular profit? I mentioned in Chapter 7 that "publicly traded brokerage house shares offer especially good opportunities for investors during the early stages of a bull market. Because their 'industry' is the stock market itself, they tend to exaggerate the movements of the stock market." And as you will learn in Chapter 9, the very best time to buy stocks is during the depth of a recession. Then you are positioned to profit from their spectacular rise, percentage-wise, during the early stages of the next bull market.

Thus you can see why I pay special attention to Merrill Lynch options during a recession. As a brokerage stock, Merrill Lynch should take off with the next bull market. That means some of its call options should do even better. I think a ten-to-one return is a good bet with some decent timing. And with the right luck, who knows—you may emulate the Financial Armadillo I mentioned in the Preface, whose $8,750 investment in Merrill Lynch options grew to $405,125 in only thirteen weeks.

Now, *that's* a winning ticket in any lottery!

· Part III ·
THE FINANCIAL ARMADILLO'S SURVIVAL INSTINCT— A KEEN SENSE OF TIMING

· NINE ·

What the Financial Armadillo Must Know About the Business Cycle

Successful investing is the art of properly utilizing probability. You want the odds to be in your favor when you make your major moves. You don't expect to win every battle, but you do aim to win the war—to realize an ever-increasing net worth for your investment portfolio.

With this overall aim in mind, you want to do everything possible to increase your probabilities of success, not to lower them. One of the best ways to do this is to make your investment moves with the business cycle foremost in mind. If you know when to get into the stock market and when to get out, you've got most of the war won. And it's the business cycle that tells you when to get in and out of the stock market.

Each business cycle has three general, but distinct stages:

Stage 1 is the growth stage of the cycle. Out of the depths of a recession or depression, the economy begins to grow, and the growth is often surprisingly swift.

Stage 2 is the period of consolidation. The economy is still vibrant, but the *momentum* of its growth is heading down.

Stage 3 is the return to recession. The economy now shrinks rather than grows, and the new recession signals the completion of this business cycle.

The Single Most Important Thing
I Can Tell You About the Stock Market

The stock market is directly tied to the state of the economy—the business cycle. It does well when the economy is growing, and does poorly when the economy turns back toward recession.

That may seem so "obvious" that you wonder why I bother to make the point. Well, I make the point because most investors forget these most elementary facts when they get emotionally involved in their investments. They keep trying to make a killing in the stock market when the business cycle tells them they should get out and place their money elsewhere. And they often let their very best opportunities for the best possible profits pass them by.

I don't want you to do that. Therefore, keep your eye on the ball—the business cycle—and pay special attention to my next paragraph. In fact, copy it and place it where you will see it every time you turn to your investments and make your next decision.

The single most important thing I can tell you about the stock market is simply this: Major stock market advances come out of recessions. Therefore, you want to move heavily *into* the stock market when things are gloomiest—during periods of recession when the headlines tell of long unemployment lines, layoffs, and poor retail sales. The other side of the coin, of course, is that you want to get *out* of the stock market while the economic news is still good, and before it turns sour. Do this and you will make your biggest possible profits and cut your losses. You will have placed the odds on your side.

Mind you, I am not talking about in-and-out trading. Leave that to the professionals who can afford to lose their shirts. I am talking about *primary* shifts in the stock market, not the minor twists and turns. If you can master the art of detecting those primary shifts before they occur—and I'll show you how in this chapter—you will do much better, most of the time, than 90 percent of those frenetic traders.

Trading in and out of the stock market is fun, and can occasionally even be profitable, if you have excess funds to play with. For your basic portfolio, however, trading is simply not an advisable strategy for individual investors. Our economy and monetary system are far too huge and complex to allow financially beneficial short-term forecasts of the stock market. Moreover, (1) emotions tend to rule the day, (2) gains are taxed as ordinary income, (3) the considerable value of dividend and capital gains compounding goes down the drain, and (4) brokerage commissions quickly eat into your profits.

Learn to be capital gains oriented. Key your stock market decisions to the major cycles of the economy, and accordingly plan to revise your holdings every two or three years. Good things don't last forever.

Getting In

Since World War II, there have been ten separate bull markets in the United States. With just one exception (the bull market of the late 1970s), every bull market started during a period of recession or during periods of clear economic distress. The longest runs were the three-year bull markets of 1949–53 and 1962–65, and the four-year bull market of 1983–86 (I am writing this portion of the book in late 1986). The shortest bull market was the one-year bull market of 1961.

It is quite clear that major advances in the stock market will begin only when business is bad and the mood of the public is quite negative. Bull markets are not kicked off during the good times.

Look for the government's quarterly reports on the gross national product (GNP). These reports are widely publicized in the press and on television, so you won't have any trouble keeping abreast of this information. A recession is officially defined as two or more quarters, back to back, of negative real GNP.

Once the GNP has been down for one quarter, therefore, you should begin your homework as to how and where you want to invest in the stock market (see Chapters 6 to 8). When the GNP has been down for two consecutive quarters, start making your moves. As a general rule, bear markets last for twelve to twenty months. It is rare for downswings to last much longer, and only during the sharp 1962 downswing was the bear market completed in much under a year. After six months of economic contraction, therefore, you can expect stock prices to be near their bottoms. You certainly won't find more attractive prices once the tide turns back up.

Getting Out

Getting *into* the stock market is a relatively easy matter. You will know when the country is in the depths of a recession, no doubt about it. Getting *out,* however, is a much more difficult matter of timing. The timespan for bull markets varies much more than for bear markets, and there often are false signals— temporary plateaus or downswings—before the bull market has truly been completed.

This is probably the most difficult decision-making process you will encounter as an investor. Because of its complexity, I have devoted much time and effort to this matter—time and effort that have resulted in the construction of my Market Tension Index (MTI). The details of how it works are proprietary information; you have to subscribe to one of my publications to get my readings. I would be remiss in my obligations to you, the reader, however, if I did not inform you of this service. I will also give you nine other tools you can use on your own. While not as sophisticated as my MTI, they go a long way toward helping you to tell when the economy and the stock market are about to change in a fundamental way.

Dick Young's Market Tension Index (MTI)

Interest rates shape the economy and the stock market to a degree unmatched by any other single factor. Accordingly, my Market Tension Index (MTI) is keyed specifically to interest rates.

Interest rates are so vitally important because they represent the cost of using money, and money is the lubricant of business, of the stock market, of the entire economy. If you are borrowing money, the amount you have to pay for the use of that money (the interest rate on your loan) is of obvious concern. But even if you don't have to borrow money, interest rates should concern you. You will be weighing the return you could get by loaning your money to someone else (such as to the U.S.

government, by buying Treasury securities) versus the return you could get from other investments.

Long-term interest rates peak during periods of recession. Short-term interest rates peak a little before a recession, or even during the strongest phase of economic recovery, before the economy actually turns down. This has been the case over the last twenty or thirty years. The stock market hates advances in interest rates (increases in the cost of using money), and particularly rapid increases. You can see, then, why the stock market does so poorly in a time of recession. On the other hand, the stock market thrives on interest rates that decline, *and decline rapidly*. Thus it is that the growth phase of the business cycle (Stage 1) is marked by declining interest rates and an advancing stock market.

As my proxy for the entire stock market, I watch the Standard & Poor's 500 Common Stock Index (the "S&P 500"). I have used it for well over a decade and have found it to be an excellent guide to major turning points in the stock market as a whole. An advance in the S&P 500 signifies an advance in the stock market as a whole; a decline in the S&P 500 correspondingly signifies a decline in the stock market as a whole.

My Market Tension Index, then, is a guide to what's going to happen to the S&P 500 and, by inference, to the entire stock market. The MTI tells you when the climate for the stock market is good and when the climate is dangerous for stock investments.

To do its job, my MTI tracks seven key interest rates. They are:

1. *The federal funds rate.* This is probably the most important of the seven rates, since it serves as the rudder of the interest rate system. Quite simply, it is the rate at which banks loan to each other overnight. It is a professional's lending rate; you do not go to your bank and say "I would like to borrow money at the federal funds rate."

2. *The discount rate.* At any point in time, banks have the option of borrowing in the open market or borrowing from the Federal Reserve. The discount rate is the rate at which they borrow from the Federal Reserve.

Next we go to to the enormous Treasury securities market, using three rates—a short-term rate, a medium-term rate, and a long-term rate.

3. *The rate on ninety-day Treasury bills.*
4. *The rate on five-year Treasury notes.*
5. *The rate on long-term Treasury bonds.*
6. *The ninety-day CD rate.* "CD" stands for "certificate of deposit." However, we're not talking about your local bank CDs, but rather the six-figure ($100,000 or more) institutional CDs. This rate serves as a check on the ninety-day Treasury bill rate, in case something causes the T-bill rate to be temporarily out of phase.
7. *The prime rate.* In theory, if not always in practice, this is the rate at which banks loan to their biggest and best customers. While it has its detractors, the prime rate still serves as a flagship rate for judging the trend of business lending. It also receives considerable press, so it is both an easy and a useful rate to use.

I check these seven rates every day, usually before 8:00 A.M. I test them *eight ways* each day—for *direction, momentum,* and *divergence.*

Direction has already been discussed. We saw that as a general rule, declining interest rates provide a positive environment for stocks, and rising interest rates point to a negative environment. But that's only a general rule. If you chart the S&P 500 against the prime rate or any other interest rate, you will see periods when their directions differ. So my MTI also tests the seven rates for momentum and divergence.

Momentum is a key way to spot a reversal of trends in advance. If interest rates have been dropping rapidly, then begin to stabilize, this loss of momentum can be a sign that the main trend is about to reverse itself—that interest rates will soon start to rise. The reverse is also true. A loss of momentum in interest rate hikes may indicate that interest rates will soon stabilize and then start declining.

Divergence is the difference between short-term and longer-term rates. As a rule, the stock market does poorly whenever short-term rates are higher than long-term rates (this is called an "inverse yield curve"). This is usually true no matter what the *level* of interest rates is, and whether the trend is up or down. Conversely, the stock market tends to do well whenever long-term money is more expensive than short-term money. Therefore, my MTI is designed to consider the divergence in rates of different terms.

I mentioned that I give *eight tests daily* to these seven interest rates, tests that measure their direction, momentum, and divergence. Each individual test is graded as having a positive or negative influence on the S&P 500. Positive readings add a point to the MTI, while negative readings do not add a point. Thus, the MTI could read anywhere from 0 to 8, although readings of either 0 or 8 are rare.

An MTI reading of 6, 7, or 8 means there are good times ahead for the stock market. A reading of 0, 1, 2, or 3 is negative. MTI readings of 4 or 5 point to a transition in the climate for the stock market, and in that case you pay attention to whether the trend in the MTI readings has been up or down.

How Well Does the MTI Work?

I have calculated the MTI daily since 1971, and less frequently since the late 1960s. In all that time, the MTI has never failed to signal a major shift in the S&P 500 and, by extension, in the stock market. It has worked so well that I have not had to revise my methods once.

You don't have to take my word for it, though. This is what *Professional Investor,* an independent service, has to say about my MTI: "Suffice to say that we have in our possession the documented record of this indicator [MTI] going back to 1965, and it has not missed any of the major turns since 1965."

The stock market boomed in the second half of 1982, catching most investors off guard. Then it died in mid-1983. Did my MTI catch those moves? This is what *Money* magazine told its readers in its May 1984 issue: "Young's advice on stocks also has been timely. In July 1982 he correctly forecast a stock market rise. A year ago, after prices had climbed more than 50 percent, he warned his subscribers to look elsewhere for profits. Such predictions, based largely on his daily study of interest rates and their impact on financial markets, have won Young, 43, a sterling reputation among [his] subscribers."

Finally, did my MTI give advance warning on the record stock market highs of 1985? Turning again to *Professional Investor,* its May 24, 1985, review answers this question best: "Two indicators that have been unusually (almost incredibly) reliable for the last two years, are both roaringly bullish now (and correctly predicted the recent breakout above 1,300). These are: Dick Young's Market Tension Index and Art Merrill's Second Hour Index. They continue to predict further gains."

The autumn of 1985 was another period that caught many "money managers"* off guard; they became "nervous Nellies" because of the length of the stock market boom, and got their clients out of the market just as it began its run past 1400, then 1500, then 1600 (in 1986) and 1700 on the Dow Jones industrial average.

Was I part of that unhappy bunch? Not at all. With my MTI as my guide, I had a full "buy" signal from April 1985 through all those spectacular gains in late 1985 and early 1986.

That's enough tooting of my own horn. You can obtain my MTI readings (and even call a special telephone number to obtain the MTI readings daily) by subscribing to one of my newsletters or reports. Full information is found in Chapter 12, "The Well-Informed Financial Armadillo."

Nine More Tools You Can Use to Forecast Basic Shifts in the Stock Market

Now let's proceed to look at nine other ways *you*—on your own—can forecast the future direction of the stock market. While these tools are not as comprehensive or sophisticated as my MTI, they can help you enormously. Instead of relying on the mob psychology of the financial markets, you can use these nine tests to get an objective indication of where the market is headed. They are not infallible, of course, but they can put you far ahead of the crowd and place the odds in your favor.

Tool No. 1: The Industrial Production Index

This is perhaps your single most important tool in forecasting the direction of the economy and the stock market. Moreover, it is simple to work with and is easily found each month. With this tool you don't have to be a professional economist to have a

---

*I like the definition of a "money manager" as "someone who manages your money until it's all gone."

pretty good idea of where you stand in the business cycle.

Each month the board of governors of the Federal Reserve System publishes its "Index of Industrial Production (Seasonally Adjusted)." This index is usually released on the 16th or 17th of each month, and you will find full coverage in the *Wall Street Journal* and major metropolitan newspapers. If the 16th and 17th fall on a weekend, the *Journal*'s story will probably appear on the 18th.

Since the 1940s, industrial production has been a good proxy of overall economic activity. Unlike GNP numbers, which are released quarterly (every three months), the industrial production figures have the advantage of being released on a monthly basis. Yes, the government does revise its figures sometimes, but usually the revisions are not deep.

The Federal Reserve breaks down industrial production figures into these categories:

Total
    Consumer goods
    Business equipment
    Defense and space
Manufacturing only
    Durable goods
    Nondurable goods [items lasting less than three years]
Mining
Utilities

That gives you an idea of what the index covers, but you need be concerned only with the "total" figure. And what you want to do with that figure is to construct a chart. Each month, on that chart, you will note how much the index has increased or decreased from the index for a year earlier. You will find this information in the *Wall Street Journal* story.

As I write, for example, the industrial production index for May 1986 has risen 0.5 percent above the index for May 1985. You mark "+0.5%" on your chart for May 1986.

What you are doing, in this way, is charting the growth or decline of the economy—and not only the direction of change, but the momentum of that change. This is critically important.

When the index is above year-ago levels and moving *increasingly higher,* you can be certain the economy is on good footing, so you can continue to be aggressive in your stock market investments.

When the index is still above year-ago levels but the monthly gains are getting smaller, you are losing momentum. Declining production momentum points to a weakening economy, so you should be more cautious in your financial planning. As the momentum gets smaller and smaller, you have a good indication that the stock market is near its peak. You will want to start taking your profits and place them in safe investments, such as Treasury bills, that will be more stable as the economy increasingly turns sour.

Bear in mind that once momentum in the industrial production index begins to turn down, interest rates begin to turn up in a cyclical sense. Why is that? Well, when momentum is lost in the economy, the easy part of a business cycle for corporate cash flow begins to slide a bit and corporate America, in general, goes back to the banks to borrow. The increased competition for the available money causes interest rates to start to turn up. This is a very basic concept at work.

Once industrial production is *below* year-ago levels, a recession is a real risk. It won't become a recession officially until there have been two consecutive quarters of declining GNP, but this is your early warning signal. Now you really want to pack your bags and get out of the stock market.

What range can you expect to see in this monthly comparison with year-ago levels? Over many cycles, I have found that the rate of change will vary from around −17 percent to around +15 percent. In other words, at the worst part of a recession industrial production may be 17 percent less than it was a year before. And at the height of a boom, industrial production may be as much as 15 percent above what it was a year earlier.

These numbers do not jump all over the map, from month to month. You will not find a figure of +10 percent one month and −10 percent the next month. That is the beauty of using these year-to-year numbers. You get a smooth trend that you can look at for indications of change. And you are getting *history*, not projections into the future that might very well prove wrong. These figures show you where you were a year ago and where you are now, and from the historical nature of the business cycle you can use these figures to project what is coming next.

For most investors, the monthly stories in the *Wall Street Journal* and other newspapers are all that you need to use this tool. If you are a student with a specialized interest in the economy, however, you may wish to write to the Board of Governors, Federal Reserve System, Washington, D.C. 20551, and ask to be placed on the mailing list of the Fed's G.12.3 industrial production release.

Tool No. 2: Commercial and Industrial Loan Demand

In our discussion of Tool No. 1, the industrial production index, we noted that corporations have to increase their borrowing as economic growth slows down; that this increased demand for money causes interest rates to rise; and that the rising rates have a further negative effect on the economy and the stock market.

Tool No. 2 will help you corroborate this trend by giving you up-to-date information on business loan demand. As your source, you can use the chart and tables titled "Business Loans (Commercial and Industrial)." You will find this on the last page of the weekly publication, *U.S. Financial Data,* available without charge from the Federal Reserve Bank of St. Louis, P.O. Box 442, St. Louis, MO 63166.

The figure you want, as with Tool No. 1, is the comparison with year-ago levels. You will find this information on the upper left corner of the chart. For example, I am looking at the issue of *U.S. Financial Data* dated September 11, 1986. In the upper left corner of the "Business Loans" chart, I read: "Compounded annual rates of change, average of the four weeks ending August 27, 1986, from the four weeks ending: . . ." I go down the dates until I come to the year-ago data: "August 28, 1985: 1.3%." What this tells me is that business demand for loans as of August 27, 1986 was 1.3 percent higher than it was a year earlier.

Keep a chart of these weekly numbers. If the trend in year-to-year numbers is down, the trend in interest rates will probably be down, and you can expect business and the stock market to do well. If loan demand picks up dramatically, the potential for a new wave of interest rate hikes is in place, and that will cause problems for the economy and the stock market.

Over many cycles, the year-to-year growth rate in commercial and industrial loans will tend to peak above 20 percent.

With that perspective, you can use your current trend figures to determine where you stand in the interest rate cycle.

Tool No. 3: The Divergence Between the Ninety-Day CD Rate and the Prime Rate

Keep track of the difference between the prime rate and the ninety-day CD rate. As long as the difference is above two percentage points, there is a prospect for additional cuts in the prime rate, and that would likely be bullish for the stock market. When the difference between the two rates is less than two percent, there is little likelihood for further cuts in the prime. Instead there may be an increase in the prime, with a depressing effect on the stock market.

Why is this so? Because the ninety-day CD rate is the rate at which banks themselves have to borrow much of their money. And the prime rate is the cheapest rate at which the banks, in turn, lend money to their best business customers.

Two percent happens to be the stress point between these two rates—the profit margin the banks generally require. As the gap widens from 2 percent to 2.5 percent, there is pressure on the banking system to lower the prime rate, because its cost of obtaining funds at the ninety-day CD rate is declining. On the other hand, when the difference falls below 1.75 percent, the banks will be paying more to obtain funds and will eventually be forced to raise the prime in order to maintain their profit margins.

Remember: When the prime lending rate is declining, stock prices are normally going up and the U.S. economic climate is usually bright. When the prime begins to head up, stock prices tend to decline and business eventually turns down because of the high cost of borrowing.

To find these rates, look in the "Money Rates" box in the second section of the *Wall Street Journal*. It is usually on or near the page with the "Credit Markets" feature article by Tom Herman and Edward P. Foldessy.

Tool No. 4: Inflation-Adjusted Growth of "High-Powered Money"

"High-powered money" is my colloquial term for what the economists call the "adjusted monetary base." Quite simply, it is the cash or currency in people's pockets, plus bank reserves. For a more detailed description of high-powered money, see Chapter 10 ("What the Financial Armadillo Must Know About Inflation," pages 183–185). There we use the growth rate in high-powered money as a sign of future inflation. We will see that a long-term growth rate above 9 percent leads to serious inflationary problems down the road.

Here we want to use the growth rate in high-powered money as a tool for forecasting the economy. To do that, we have to know the growth rate in high-powered money *and* the current twelve-month consumer price index (CPI)—the rate of consumer price inflation. The CPI is released monthly by the government and reported widely in the press. Keep a running chart of each month's CPI when it appears in the press.

What we will do is take the growth rate in high-powered money and subtract the CPI. This gives us the *real* (inflation-adjusted) rate of growth in high-powered money. The U.S. economy will continue to expand as long as the real (inflation-adjusted) rate of growth in high-powered money is positive (above 0). The history of the past fifteen years indicates that there is little likelihood of a full-scale recession as long as we have real growth in high-powered money.

On the other hand, a recession is a good prospect when the real rate of growth in high-powered money turns negative—that is, when the CPI is greater than the nominal rate of growth in high-powered money. Bear in mind that this can happen because of (1) too little growth in high-powered money, (2) too much inflation, or (3) a combination of the two.

So, how do we find the rate of growth in high-powered money? We turn to the same publication we used for Tool No. 2 —*U.S. Financial Data*, published weekly by the Federal Reserve Bank of St. Louis. On page 2 you will find the chart for "Adjusted Monetary Base," and below the chart will be a table with the figures we want. For example, see Table 15 from the June 26, 1986, issue, which follows on page 172.

This tells us that the current 12-month rate of growth in high-powered money is 8.1 percent. That's the rate of growth from June 19, 1985, to June 18, 1986. The most recent (June 1986) Consumer Price Index is 1.7 percent. This means that the *real* rate of growth in high-powered money is 6.4 percent (8.1–1.7). That's positive and points to continued growth in the economy.

TABLE 15
Adjusted Monetary Base
(June 26, 1986)

TO THE AVERAGE OF TWO MAINTENANCE PERIODS ENDING:	COMPOUNDED ANNUAL RATES OF CHANGE, AVERAGE OF TWO MAINTENANCE PERIODS ENDING:							
	6/19/85	9/11/85	11/20/85	12/18/85	1/15/86	2/12/86	3/12/86	4/23/86
11/20/85	6.9							
12/18/85	8.0	6.9						
1/15/86	7.3	6.0	8.4					
2/12/86	7.2	6.0	7.7	4.5				
3/12/86	7.8	7.1	8.9	7.2	9.5			
4/23/86	7.3	6.6	7.7	6.3	7.3	7.7		
5/21/86	7.6	7.1	8.3	7.2	8.2	8.8	7.2	
6/18/86	8.1	7.7	9.0	8.2	9.2	9.8	9.0	12.5

Tool No. 5: The Index of Twelve Leading Indicators

Each month the Commerce Department's Bureau of Economic Analysis issues its "Composite Index of Twelve Leading Indicators." These leaders live up to their name: they are timely indicators of cyclical change in the U.S. economy.

The S&P 500 is itself one of the government's twelve leading indicators. The others are M-2 money supply, change in credit outstanding (business and consumer borrowing), change in sensitive materials prices, net change in inventories, contracts for plant and equipment, new building permits, average weekly claims for state unemployment insurance, average workweek of production workers, net orders for consumer goods and materials, vendor performance (companies receiving slower deliveries from suppliers), and net business formation. You can see how items such as these would signal major changes in the economy.

What you want to look for is each month's "composite index reading"—in May 1986 it was 178.8, for example—and whether this is above or below the reading for a year earlier. Keep a record of each month's reading and its change from a year earlier.

During periods of economic expansion, the leaders may advance to a level as much as 20 percent above prior-year levels.

In periods of recession, the leaders may fall as much as 10 percent below prior-year levels. Moreover, you can use the leaders to warn you in advance of changes in the business cycle.

Recession

The index of leading indicators always turns down in a recession. There has been no exception. Once your monthly readings are below year-ago levels, a recession is likely.

Have the leaders ever declined sharply without a subsequent recession? Yes, twice—in 1951 and 1966. But note that those were both years of general economic distress, even though they did not officially qualify as recessions.

The problem is that the downturn by the leaders has led recession by as few as three months and as many as twenty-three months. For this reason, it would be a mistake to rely solely on the leading indicators as an early warning guide to recession. But you certainly *can* expect the leaders to turn down before you get the next recession.

Recovery

Here the leaders have performed with a great deal more consistency and accuracy. The leaders have turned up in advance of every economic recovery since 1948. Furthermore, their lead time has been in a fairly compressed range of one to eight months. In fact, from 1955 through 1980—a time period spanning five recessions—the lead time was either one or two months.

Once you see the leaders go up, therefore (and by "up" I mean above year-ago levels), you want to move quickly into the stock market if you have not done so already. There is no more time to lose if you want to take advantage of the stock market's rise with the economy.

Where do you find the monthly reading of the index of leading indicators? Near the beginning of each month, the government releases its data for two months earlier. In early December, for example, it will release the data for October. This information is reported thoroughly in the *Wall Street Journal* and major metropolitan newspapers, even small newspapers.

You can also obtain the data by subscribing to the government's monthly *Business Conditions Digest* (*BCD*), or by referring to this publication at a local library. For subscription information write to the Superintendent of Documents, U.S. Government Printing Office, Washington, D.C. 20402. The index of leading economic indicators is always item No. 910 in each month's *BCD*.

Tool No. 6: The Index of Four
Coincident Indicators

This index tracks nonagricultural employment, personal income (less transfer payments) in 1972 dollars, industrial production, and manufacturing and trade sales in 1972 dollars.

With these coincident indicators, year-to-year momentum offers the best overall guidance to the economy. Over the last twenty years they have risen to 12 or 13 percent above prior-year levels, then fallen below the zero reference point.

Watch for a year-to-year decline that takes the coincidents to a level 5 percent *or lower* above the year-ago level. We can go back to the late 1940s and find instances where such declines have foretold recession. Once year-to-year figures fall *below 5 percent on the plus side,* recession or economic contraction lies directly ahead.

The index of coincident indicators is always item No. 920 in *Business Conditions Digest.* New figures are released monthly by the Commerce Department, along with the leading indicators.

Tool No. 7: The Ratio of Deflated Inventories
to Sales

Tools 7 and 8 are secondary tools—not as important as the ones we have already discussed, but useful collaborators.

The government's official label for Tool No. 7 is "Ratio, Constant-Dollar Inventories to Sales, Manufacturing, and Trade." This ratio is expressed as the number 1 and a fraction carried to two decimal points. A ratio of 1.65, for example, means that for the United States as a whole, businesses have 1.65 units of merchandise in inventory for each unit of merchandise sold.

If you think about that ratio, you will understand what happens next. Sales are brisk in good times, so in times of economic growth inventories are relatively low. The ratio will portray this situation. In the best of times you can expect the ratio to go as low as 1.5. That point has been reached only three times since

1956. They were periods of strong economic growth and stock market peaks.

On the other hand, sales fall off in periods of recession. The shelves are full of unsold goods. The ratio, therefore, also rises in periods of recession. It has advanced to 1.7 four times since 1956. It has gone as high as 1.8. Therefore, 1.5 to 1.8 is the range you can expect to see in this ratio.

How to use this ratio? Well, when it declines to 1.5, you can figure that the best times are over. You are somewhere near the peak of economic growth and stock market strength, and it is time to pull out. At the other end of the range, when this ratio goes to 1.7 you can figure the economy has bottomed and will soon bounce back up. It's time to get back into the stock market.

You will find the ratio listed as item No. 77 in each month's *Business Conditions Digest*.

Tool No. 8: The Ratio of Personal Income to Money Supply

This is what economists would call a measure of the "velocity" of money. Velocity is the rate at which money is spent—in other words, how many times a dollar is spent in a certain period of time. We get this particular measure, or ratio, by dividing the personal income of Americans by the M-2 money supply.

If the Federal Reserve increases the money supply fast, that's usually positive for the economy. (We are talking here about immediate stimulation of the economy, ignoring long-term inflationary effects.) People have more spending power. If it tightens up on the money supply, the reverse is true—the economy tends to contract.

We are dividing personal income by the M-2 money supply to get this ratio. The greater the money supply, therefore, the lower the number in this ratio. Using this ratio, then, remember that downward trends in the ratio point to economic growth, and upward trends in the ratio point to eventual contraction and recession.

Over a thirty-year period of time, this ratio has ranged between 1.24 and 1.48. The ratio becomes negative—it points to bad times—once it goes above 1.35 in the direction of the maximum 1.48.

By charting this ratio each month and noting the trend, you can tell whether the economy is nearing its peak or heading for its bottom, and make your investment decisions accordingly. You will find the ratio of personal income to money supply as item No. 108 in the *Business Conditions Digest.*

Tool No. 9: The Quadrennial Theory

The quadrennial theory basically says that a presidential election year and the year preceding it will tend to be good years for the stock market. And the two years following a presidential election tend to be less good or not good for the stock market.

That doesn't sound like a very "scientific" theory until you think about it. What is the first goal of every politician? To get re-elected, of course. And how do they do that? By passing out the goodies—handouts and benefits of every possible description. The presidency is the number 1 prize in our political system, so the goodies are flowing like crazy as we head for another presidential election.

Politicians much prefer to hand out any bad-tasting medicine *after* they get elected. That's why the two years after a presidential election tend, on balance, to be worse ones for the stock market. And it explains why the party in power tends to suffer setbacks in the first congressional elections after their presidential victory. This is true whether we are talking about Democrats or Republicans. Both try to save the desserts for the next presidential campaign.

The important point is that history reinforces the validity of this theory. I certainly would not base my investments on this theory alone, but the quadrennial theory does offer an overall perspective that makes sense out of what all these statistics tell you.

Ten Tools to Use and Three "Sins" to Overcome if You Want to Be a Successful Investor

Did you ever imagine that you have this many tools available for charting the probable course of the economy and the stock market?

I have given you ten. You can subscribe to one of my publications and receive regular updates of my Market Tension Index. Or you can use the other nine tools on your own. All it will take is about an hour of your time each week, using the *Wall Street Journal* or your daily newspaper, the St. Louis Fed's *U.S. Financial Data,* and the Commerce Department's *Business Conditions Digest.* Better yet, subscribe to one of my publications *and* check me out by also using the other nine tools!

Keep in mind that none of these tools is infallible. But the more of them you use, the more accurate a reading you are going to get. Bear in mind, too, that these tools won't forecast every twist and turn in the market. Use them to chart the *major cyclical turns* in the economy and the stock market, and plan your investments accordingly.

If this much hard information is available to anyone who wants to use it, and if it is this reliable, then why do so many people continue to do so poorly—or even lose their shirts—when it comes to their investments? Let me suggest three reasons.

Greed

Too many investors are too anxious to get every possible dollar before they sell or switch investments. They are determined to sell *at* the very peak rather than *near* the peak, and we know what the result usually is: They get burned, holding that particular investment until it is cascading downhill.

You cannot separate the American economy from the rest of the world's economy, and today's worldwide economy is far too large and far too complex to allow anyone to predict its exact moves. The government, with all its computers and statisticians and planners, cannot do it; how will you? Be content to have an accurate outline of the big picture.

Laziness

I am referring to mental laziness as much as physical laziness here. After all, how much work is involved with these ten tools? We are talking about one hour a week maximum, at home or in the library. Isn't a secure retirement nest egg worth that much (that little!) time? But be honest as you ask yourself how many of the people you know would actually put in this minimal effort.

Peer Pressure

Other writers refer to this as the "psychology of the mob"—the investment "mob," in this instance. I prefer to use a more contemporary term. We like to point the finger at our children and lament how they give in to peer pressure, but don't we adults do the same? Aren't we much more likely to base our investment decisions on "hot tips," on a hard sell from our broker, or our "feeling" about what's going to happen with the market? And isn't that "feeling" usually shaped by the headlines we've read, the commentary we saw on television, the money talk with our fellow workers at the office?

Yes, statistics are cold and impersonal. But that's their immense value when it comes to investing your hard-earned money. By all means, learn as much as you can by watching the business news and commentaries on television, by reading the financial press, by talking to friends and business associates and perhaps even the other members of your local investment club. But then take what you hear and check it out with what these ten tools tell you is actually happening in the economy right now, and is likely to happen tomorrow.

These ten tools represent past history and future probability. By using them, you are putting the odds on *your* side.

· TEN ·

What the Financial Armadillo Must Know About Inflation

When most people think about inflation, they have in mind *price inflation*—a rise in the prices of items they buy, whether these are daily necessities (such as food in the supermarket) or infrequent major purchases (such as an automobile). The best-known gauge for measuring these price increases is the Consumer Price Index (CPI).

Economists like to be more precise, and they differentiate between monetary inflation and price inflation,* or between different stages of price inflation. This may seem like useless academic quibbling to you, since it's the end result—consumer price increases—that you are most concerned about in everyday life. As an *investor,* though, you can increase your profits dramatically by learning some simple ways to tell exactly where you stand in the inflation cycle, and whether you can expect the inflation rate to increase or decrease in the future.

For one thing, as we saw in Chapter 3, gold is the premier hedge against inflation. This makes it extremely important to be able to discern where you stand in the inflation cycle. The very best time to increase your gold holdings is when the inflation rate has bottomed, for that's when gold prices have likely bottomed as well. You will still find excellent buying opportunities during the early stages of the new inflationary cycle, but your risk increases as inflation becomes more pronounced. If you are

---

*See my story illustrating monetary inflation and price inflation in Chapter 3, pages 63–64.

too heavily invested in gold when inflation crests and starts back down, your risk is extreme. Gold prices will soon plummet, too, following the lead of the inflationary cycle.

Interest rates are another good reason for knowing what the prospects are for inflation. Over the long run the rate of interest will directly reflect the rate of inflation. And when the inflationary cycle takes off, interest rates will tend to move higher than they normally would. Inflation is not the only factor affecting interest rates, but if you know what's going to happen with inflation, you have a powerful clue as to what's going to happen with interest rates.

And why should you be concerned about interest rates? A direct reason, of course, is the possibility that you may want or need to take out a loan. If you expect interest rates to rise, you can save money by taking out a loan *now;* conversely, if you expect interest rates to fall, it would pay to wait as long as possible before seeking your loan.

Interest rates also have a direct bearing on the value of your investments in fixed-income debt securities, such as corporate bonds or Treasury securities. These rise in value when interest rates fall, and decline in value when interest rates rise. Therefore, if you can judge what's likely to happen with inflation and interest rates, you know whether you want your holdings in debt securities to be long-term or short-term.

As you can see, there are some real advantages to knowing what's likely to happen with inflation. Moreover, you don't have to be a wizard or a professional economist to figure out the future course of inflation. I have devoted considerable time and effort to analyzing the inflationary cycle, and I have found that each new rising cycle has three distinct stages. If you learn what to look for, the first two stages can serve as "early warning signals" for the full-blown inflation that's sure to follow.

Stage 1 of the inflationary cycle falls into place when *crude materials prices* turn from a period of disinflation or low inflation to a period of increased inflationary momentum. Crude materials are unprocessed items entering the economy for the first time, so it's logical that a rise in prices will be noticed here first, and will then be felt down the line.

And that's exactly what happens. *Stage 2* of the inflationary cycle falls into place when *wholesale prices,* or *producer prices* as they are now called, begin to rise. Since raw materials are costing more, wholesalers have to raise the prices on their products to the retailers who are their customers.

Stage 3 of the inflationary cycle falls into place last, when *consumer prices* start up. Retailers have to charge you, the consumer, higher prices because their wholesale costs have risen. Accordingly, the Consumer Price Index turns from disinflation to inflation. This is the stage of the inflation cycle that provides the groundwork for booming precious metals prices, but if you paid attention to the previous stages you were able to buy your gold in advance, when prices were rock-bottom. And that, of course, is the entire key to making your biggest-possible profits: Buy low and sell high.

There are three other indicators of the future course of inflation: (1) the rate of growth of *"high-powered money,"* (2) the *underlying rate of inflation,* and (3) *real rates of interest.* Combined with the three stages of price increases, they can give you a very good portrait of the future, with no wizardry involved. Now let's see exactly how to do this.

Stage 1: Crude Materials Prices

An upward swing in inflation will show up here long before it's noticed in the supermarket. Crude materials are both food and nonfood items that are reaching the market for the first time, without any processing. In other words, they're in the rawest state possible. The U.S. Bureau of Labor Statistics provides price information for twenty-one of these crude materials, and I follow their prices rigorously. Each month, the Bureau calls me when they get the latest prices for these items out of the computer. (I've done as much work with this as anyone, which is one reason they phone this information to me immediately.)

The most important of these items are what I call the "meat and heat" group—cattle, hogs, milk, coal, gas, and oil prices. Together, they account for about 65 percent of the momentum in crude prices. Cattle prices have the single greatest impact, with oil prices second in importance. Oil prices account for about 15 percent of the total crude price momentum.

If you will look at Table 17, you will see the impact of the two huge increases in oil prices in the 1970s. The average price for crude oil in 1973 was $2.70 per barrel; this exploded to $9.76

per barrel in 1974. The second big jump came from 1978 ($12.70) to 1980 ($28.67). The double-digit price inflation of 1974 and 1979–81 was influenced strongly by these exploding oil prices.

Since mid-1980, crude prices—including cattle and oil prices—have been in a deflationary trend. Crude prices are not the only factor behind inflation, so the deflation here was not enough to spur consumer price deflation. But it was a major reason why consumer price inflation was kept under 4 percent from 1983 into 1986.

Crude prices are volatile, and many of them are affected by weather conditions. It is important, therefore, to look at the overall trend rather than each individual jump up or down, month by month.

How can you keep track of what's happening? The Bureau of Labor Statistics releases its crude materials prices each month, and I analyze these in each of my publications (see Chapter 12). If you want to do this on your own, you will find the new figures in the financial pages of major newspapers such as the *Wall Street Journal* around the middle of the month, when they are released by the Bureau of Labor Statistics.

Stage 2: Producer (Wholesale) Prices

Producer (wholesale) prices are less volatile than crude materials prices. Crude materials prices are perhaps more important to monitor, since they are your *earliest* warning of inflationary pressures in the economy. But producer price trends will confirm and refine the direction in which broad-based inflation is headed. If you see producer prices going up, you know that consumer prices—as reflected in the CPI—will soon follow, and you want to waste no time in making the appropriate investment decisions.

U.S. producer prices have not declined in any year since 1953. Producer price inflation peaked in 1979 with an annual rate of growth of over 20 percent. That inflation rate has since come down dramatically. In 1985 the annual advance was only 0.1 percent. You won't see a resurgence of consumer price inflation until there is some action here first.

The data we look for here are called "Intermediate Materials

Prices" and are released monthly by the Commerce Department. The *Wall Street Journal* and other major newspapers always cover this news.

Stage 3: Consumer Prices

This is the final stage of the inflationary process, when price increases have seeped through the economy from the raw, unprocessed state to the wholesalers, and now to the retail outlets that sell directly to you, the consumer.

As we have noted, the best-known and most widely used gauge at this stage is the Consumer Price Index, released monthly by the Commerce Department. You can count on coverage each month on TV and in major newspapers, giving the most recent CPI and related findings. If you want to get on the mailing list, write to the Bureau of Labor Statistics, U.S. Department of Labor, Washington, D.C. 20212, or call (202) 523-1913. The CPI's official title is "Percent Changes in CPI for All Urban Consumers (Seasonally Adjusted)."

"High-Powered Money"

There has been much debate and controversy in economic circles over the definitions and significance of various measurements of the amount of money in circulation—M1, M2, M3, or whatever. There's no need to go into those arcane discussions here.

There is no doubt, however, that the amount of money in circulation *is* very important in determining the tone of the economy and the course of inflation. An expanding economy needs some monetary growth—but not too much, or you'll have accelerating price inflation. And the source of that monetary growth is the Federal Reserve.

The measurement I use is formally called the "Adjusted Monetary Base." I prefer the less formal, more descriptive term "high-powered money." Whichever name you use, this is the raw material for all money creation up and down the line, and it is simply the cash or currency in people's pockets plus bank reserves. Using this measurement avoids all the controversies about M1 and the other "M's." And, if you want to see what is going to happen with inflation over any time period, you can look at the year-to-year growth in this high-powered money.

To maintain fairly stable growth in the economy, high-powered money must grow within a range of 7 to 9 percent annually. Long periods of growth above 9 percent are both rare and likely to lead to serious inflationary problems. (No full year in decades has shown growth above 10 percent.) Base growth below 7 percent is also a rarity, and points toward economic contraction or outright recession.

A little history will illustrate these points.

In 1978, we saw a long period of high-powered money growth above 9 percent. That contributed (along with the forthcoming oil price increases) to the double-digit inflation of 1979, 1980, and 1981 (see Table 17). In late 1980, the Federal Reserve began to cut the rate of monetary expansion. By November 1981 the growth rate was down to 4.4 percent, and it remained below 6 percent through May 1982. The results were a drastic cut in inflation, and the deep recession.

By 1983, the monetary authorities had again reversed gears and we had a period of growth as high as in 1978—up to 9.5 percent in September 1983, and 8.9 percent for the year. That fueled the recovery that resulted in the great stock market boom of 1983–86. By itself it also would have pointed to price inflation, but price inflation was kept in line because of the deflation in crude materials prices and the overvalued dollar.

Now, how can you find out about the current rate of growth in high-powered money? The Federal Reserve System regularly releases two series on the monetary base, and you can use either one. One series is released by the board of governors of the Federal Reserve System, and is listed weekly in the *Wall Street Journal*. The second series is released weekly by the Federal Reserve Bank of St. Louis. Over short periods of time, the growth rates of the two series can and do differ, because of the different methods they use. But over longer periods, the factors that cause the two series to differ over the short term cancel out. As a result, six-month or longer growth rates tend to be the same.

I use the St. Louis series. It is found on page 2 of its weekly publication, *U.S. Financial Data*. Here is a sample table from the August 21, 1986, issue:

TABLE 16
Adjusted Monetary Base
(August 21, 1986)

TO THE AVERAGE OF TWO MAINTENANCE PERIODS ENDING:	COMPOUNDED ANNUAL RATES OF CHANGE, AVERAGE OF TWO MAINTENANCE PERIODS ENDING:							
	8/14/85	11/6/85	1/15/86	2/12/86	3/12/86	4/9/86	5/7/86	6/18/86
1/15/86	7.2							
2/12/86	7.0	7.2						
3/12/86	7.8	8.4	9.5					
4/9/86	7.5	7.9	8.2	9.1				
5/7/86	7.4	7.7	7.8	8.3	6.1			
6/18/86	8.2	8.7	9.2	9.8	9.0	10.4		
7/16/86	8.0	8.4	8.7	9.1	8.3	9.1	10.1	
8/13/86	7.8	8.1	8.2	8.6	7.8	8.3	8.8	5.7

At that time, the current annual rate of growth (August 14, 1985, to August 13, 1986) was 7.8 percent. This was well within the "normal" range of 7 to 9 percent, indicating no significant pressures for rising inflation.

To get on the mailing list for this publication, write to the Federal Reserve Bank of St. Louis, P.O. Box 442, St. Louis, MO 63166.

The Underlying Rate of Inflation

Another way of checking the prospects for price inflation is to determine the underlying rate of inflation. We get this by taking the growth rate in average hourly earnings for production workers, and adjusting that figure for the rate of productivity.

Obviously, wage increases are not inflationary if they are matched by increases in productivity. They are inflationary, however, when they exceed growth in productivity.

Over many cycles, average hourly earnings will generally advance on a year-to-year basis within a range of 3 to 11 percent. Productivity tends to range between a negative 3 percent and a positive 6 percent. Thus in the very best of times (low wage increases and substantial gains in productivity) the underlying rate of inflation might actually be a deflationary (negative) 3 percent.

Gold prices zoom, however, on bad news—in this case, rising wages and declining productivity. During the 1975–79 period, when gold had its huge run-up, productivity was taking a nose dive.

In recent years the big story has been the collapse of union power and, with it, consistently smaller wage increases. During 1980, average hourly earnings advanced at a rate of 9 to 10 percent. By late 1981, they were increasing by only 6 to 7 percent. By mid-1982 that rate had fallen to 5 percent, and by the end of 1982 average hourly earnings were growing by only 4.5 percent. Since then wage growth has fallen even lower, and when rising productivity is taken into account, the underlying rate of inflation has been near zero and sometimes negative. There has been no trend toward inflation here.

The government's wage and productivity figures are reported in the *Wall Street Journal* and other major newspapers each month. If, for example, wages are up 5 percent and productivity is up 4 percent, the underlying rate of inflation is 1 percent.

Real Rates of Interest

This is simple. To get the *real* interest rate, you just subtract the rate of price inflation (the CPI) from the interest rate you are charting. The interest rate I use is the ninety-day Treasury bill rate.

Negative real interest rates point to inflationary pressures in the economy. As hedges against inflation, gold and silver markets *love* negative real interest rates. Negative interest rates mean that you are not getting any real return on money instruments such as T-bills when you take inflation into account. Conversely, it makes it cheap to own non-interest-bearing investments such as gold and silver.

High real interest rates, on the other hand, are very bearish for gold and silver markets. You're not earning any of that high interest with the money you have invested in metals. Indeed, if you borrow to buy your metals, you have to *pay* a high rate of interest.

From 1974 through 1980, when the price of gold soared, T-bill rates were frequently negative when adjusted for inflation (again see Table 17). Since 1980 the situation has been just the opposite. Real interest rates have been among the highest in history.

Ironically, since gold prices thrive on inflation, it appears to be the fear of renewed inflation that is keeping real interest rates so high. The historical norm for the real rate of return from T-bills has been 0 to 2.5 percent. Since 1980 the real rate of return on T-bills has ranged from 4 to 7 percent. The U.S. Treasury markets apparently do not believe inflation is dead, just lying low for a while.

Fine-Tuning Your Crystal Ball

I have given you six key indicators of the future course of inflation:

1. Crude materials prices—Stage 1 of the inflationary cycle.

2. Producer, or wholesale, prices—Stage 2 of the inflationary cycle.

3. Consumer prices—Stage 3 of the (now fully developed) inflationary cycle.

4. "High-powered money"—more formally known as the adjusted monetary base.

5. The underlying rate of inflation, or wage increases adjusted for productivity.

6. Real interest rates, or interest rates adjusted for inflation.

By keeping tabs on these six indicators, you will know as much about the future course of inflation as any of the economic gurus you see on TV or read about in the newspapers—probably more, since you will be basing your predictions on real facts, not the mob psychology of the moment. And by following more than one indicator, you are less likely to get thrown off course. Monetary growth may be high, for example, but if none of the other indicators point to renewed inflation you can discount any scare headlines you see, for now. You want to keep that monetary growth in mind, because it points to problems down the road, but you know you'll have plenty of other warnings before the inflation actually hits.

TABLE 17
Inflation in the 1970s and 1980s

YEAR	OIL ($/BARREL)	U.S. CPI	GOLD ($/OZ.)	90-DAY T-BILL RATE	REAL T-BILL YIELD	UNDERLYING RATE OF INFLATION	ANNUAL GROWTH RATE OF MONETARY BASE
1970	1.30	5.9	37.37	6.4	0.5	4.0	—
1971	1.65	4.3	43.63	4.3	0.0	3.4	7.4
1972	1.90	3.3	64.90	4.1	0.8	2.3	8.1
1973	2.70	6.3	112.25	7.0	0.7	7.1	8.0
1974	9.76	10.9	186.50	7.9	(3.0)	10.2	9.1
1975	10.72	9.2	140.25	5.8	(3.4)	3.1	7.0
1976	11.51	5.8	134.75	4.4	(1.4)	5.3	7.4
1977	12.40	6.5	164.95	6.0	(0.5)	5.6	8.7
1978	12.70	7.5	226.00	7.2	(0.3)	8.5	9.1
1979	16.97	11.3	512.00	10.0	(1.3)	9.5	8.2
1980	28.67	13.5	589.50	11.6	(1.9)	8.8	8.1
1981	32.50	10.4	397.50	14.1	3.7	7.5	5.0
1982	33.45	6.2	456.90	10.7	4.5	1.6	8.2
1983	28.60	3.8	382.40	8.9	5.1	0.0	8.9
1984	28.47	4.0	308.30	9.3	5.3	0.4	7.5
1985	28.00	3.8	327.00	7.0	3.2	2.7	8.0

The bottom line, of course, is to use this knowledge in your investment decisions. Gold and real estate will be good areas for investment during periods of increased inflation. During periods of stable inflation, the stock market tends to be a good place to be. And in those rare periods of price deflation (such as the early 1920s and 1930s), long-term U.S. government bonds offer your best bet.

·Part IV·

THE WELL-ROUNDED FINANCIAL ARMADILLO

· ELEVEN ·

When the Financial Armadillo Travels Abroad

Throughout this book I have stressed the need to diversify your assets. Don't put all your eggs in one basket. If you diversify between different types of assets and financial instruments, even a total loss in one area will not harm the rest of your portfolio.

There is another type of financial diversification that, unfortunately, is desirable in today's world. That is *geographical* diversification. This certainly is true with substantial portfolios, but it also applies to those of moderate size.

Mind you, I am not talking here about investments in foreign stocks or bonds. I am talking about having a portion of your assets physically located in or directed from a foreign country.

Geographical diversification is desirable for the same generic reason as asset diversification: You don't want all your eggs in one basket. In the geographical sense, you want most of your "eggs" close to home, where they are easily available. But having a portion of your assets in another part of the world—in an age when air travel is quick and easy—should help you sleep easier at night. It's insurance. Whatever crises hit your home port, you know you have survival funds available elsewhere.

"That's fine if you live in an unstable South American country," you protest. "But it doesn't make sense for an American. We're the foremost bastion of capitalism in the world. That's why investors around the world take out insurance by having some of their assets *here,* in the U.S.A."

Objection sustained—up to a point. I am not a doom-and-gloomer by nature, and I certainly do not ever expect to see the

Red flag flying over my home port of Newport, Rhode Island. Being prudent by nature, though, I also do not believe in acting like an ostrich or waving Old Glory as a substitute for thoughtful analysis. Yes, we have the world's largest and most bountiful economy, and it would be foolhardy not to share in the growth of that bounty. But we also have a very meddlesome government, and many of our constitutional rights have been seriously eroded, especially in the economic arena. Don't forget that these mid-1980s are "good times." What happens when bad times come? Runaway inflation, foreign exchange restrictions, wage and price controls, or the confiscation of your gold are not beyond the realm of possibility. Actions such as these have been taken before by the U.S. government, and you must allow for the possibility of their recurrence in the future.

It would be foolish, of couse, to diversify geographically by moving a portion of your assets to Haiti or the Philippines. The idea is to find a *safer haven* than the United States. Hong Kong is a great showcase for capitalism today, but who knows what will happen when the People's Republic of China takes it over in 1997? Nor do I recommend any of those "tax havens" in the Caribbean you probably have read about. A true haven is not created by the edict of a new regime that wants to attract American dollars. A true haven will have a long history of political and economic liberty, and those traditions will be so ingrained in its people that they are willing to die to maintain them.

I have just described Switzerland.

Switzerland: A Haven for All Seasons

There are specific financial reasons why I recommend Switzerland as a haven for part of your assets. Indeed, the United States can learn from tiny Switzerland when it comes to monetary stability and financial privacy. Attributes such as these do not develop in a vacuum, of course. In Switzerland's case, they rest on a firm foundation of political and economic liberty and responsibility.

The Swiss people have a well-earned reputation for hard work and frugality. They work longer hours than other Europeans; they are more productive; and the average Swiss citizen has saved more than $14,000 in addition to his or her investments. Switzerland has the highest per capita income among all industrialized nations. It has gold reserves that amount to four times the currency in circulation, and inflation is consistently low. There is no capital gains tax and there are no exchange controls (there have *never* been any restrictions on the outflow of capital from Switzerland).

On the political side, Switzerland is noted internationally for its neutrality. That neutrality, moreover, is based on a sound desire to avoid the conflicts that have devastated the rest of Europe, not because of any refusal to distinguish between right and wrong. The Swiss people themselves are firmly committed to a constitutional form of democracy, and the entire citizenry is armed and trained to repel any invasion of Swiss territory. Indeed, because of its compact size and the relative homogeneity of its population, Switzerland can practice a much more direct form of democracy than the United States. Any act of the parliament can be overturned by popular referendum, and this is often done.

For example, these are some of the decisions made by the Swiss people in recent years, by popular referenda:

• *Not* to reduce the work week by law from forty-four to forty hours.

• *Not* to increase the annual holidays by law from three weeks to four weeks.

• *Not* to levy a "windfall profits tax" on high incomes.

• *Not* to give workers a say in management.

• *Not* to allow the federal government to run deficits.

• *Not* to reduce the age for receiving benefits under the National Old Age Pension Plan.

• *Not* to give the federal government the right to raise funds to counter downturns in the economy.

• *Not* to establish a uniform tax rate for all cantons (some cantons, or provinces, have very low taxes).

Swiss Banks

Swiss banks reflect this fiscal conservatism of the nation's people. To some of our go-go bankers in the United States, their Swiss counterparts must seem very stodgy indeed. But to depositors and investors worried about the safety of their money, the Swiss banks are a model of propriety and sound financial management.

You should understand, first of all, that in Switzerland a bank is more than an institution for loans and deposits. A Swiss bank is a veritable financial supermarket. In addition to checking accounts, savings accounts, and loans, a Swiss bank is equipped to buy and sell stocks and bonds for you, to establish a corporation, to buy and store precious metals, to trade currencies and commodities, to sell life insurance annuities, and, indeed, to manage your entire portfolio for you.

Swiss banks are also very international-minded in their outlook. This is part of their heritage, since Swiss banks have served as financiers for European cities and monarchs as far back as the Middle Ages. Geography plays a role, too, with landlocked Switzerland surrounded by the major nations of Germany, France, Italy, and Austria. As a result, Swiss bankers are multilingual and intimately familiar with markets around the world.

Switzerland also has stiff liquidity and capital requirements for its banks. In Chapter 1 we saw that American banks have dangerously low liquidity levels, with 17 percent recorded in December 1985. With so few liquid assets, the U.S. banks simply are not prepared for a major run by depositors or massive defaults on their loans. This comes at a time, moreover, when they have been making increasingly huge and shaky loans to Third World countries.

Swiss banks, on the other hand, have liquidity levels that often approach or surpass 100 percent. Even a major institution such as Credit Suisse has a liquidity level of over 30 percent.

Siegfried Herzog, managing director of Zurich's Ueberseebank, adds that "Swiss private banks specialize in serving a private clientele. For that reason, we do not use deposits from our clients to go out and make risky credit judgments, either locally or on the international lending market. We live on commissions we charge for our services, not on the interest from international lending."

Swiss Banking Privacy

I have saved the best for the last. We live in an age when Big Brother's snoops are everywhere, trying to learn everything about us and our assets—the better to start confiscating, of course, should an "emergency" arise in the future. Big Brother is banished from Switzerland, though. Let's compare banking privacy in the United States and Switzerland.

United States

The Currency and Foreign Transactions Reporting Act of 1970 (the misnamed "Bank Secrecy Act of 1970") requires, among other things:

• Microfilming all checks over $100 (most banks find it more efficient to microfilm *all* checks)
• Reporting your Social Security number within 45 days of opening an account
• Reporting any transaction of $10,000 or more in cash or check, deposit or withdrawal
• Reporting any foreign transaction of $5,000 or more crossing U.S. borders.

In *Miller vs. U.S.,* the U.S. Supreme Court ruled that bank customers have "no expectation of privacy" when using a bank. "The depositor takes the risk, in revealing his affairs to another, that the information will be conveyed by that

Switzerland

Text of Article 47 of the Swiss Banking Law of Nov. 8, 1934, which was revised on March 11, 1971:
"1. Whoever divulges a secret entrusted to him in his capacity as officer, employee, authorized agent, liquidator or commissioner of a bank, as a representative of the Banking Commission, officer or employee of a recognized auditing company, or who has become aware of such a secret in this capacity, and whoever tries to induce others to violate professional secrecy, shall be punished by a prison term not to exceed six months or by a fine not exceeding Sfrs. 50,000."
"2. If the act has been committed by negligence, the penalty shall be a fine not exceeding Sfrs. 30,000."
"3. The violation of professional secrecy remains punishable even after

person to the government,"
said Justice Lewis F. Powell.

termination of the official or
employment relationship or
the exercise of the
profession."

The epitome of Swiss banking secrecy is the so-called "numbered account." Actually all accounts have numbers to identify them, but these use no name or a false name to go with the number. Since all bank accounts are kept secret from the outside world, this is just an extra veil of secrecy within the bank, popular with international celebrities and potentates. Even with these numbered accounts, the top officers of the bank have to know the identity of their holders. You don't need a numbered account.

Who Establishes a Swiss Bank Account?

The combined balance sheet of all Swiss banks—some 500 billion Swiss francs—is more than twice as large as the country's gross national product. Obviously Swiss banks are popular with a lot of people other than the Swiss themselves.

• Refugees and potential refugees from all sorts of regimes deposit their assets in Switzerland. They may already have lost their savings because of political or religious discrimination; they are determined not to let that happen again, and they know Switzerland is the safest haven because of its political neutrality, financial stability, and bank secrecy.

• Potentates of all kinds trust Switzerland with their funds. Especially if they run the risk of being deposed, they want their assets to be hidden, safe, and available after exile. Sometimes these are their legitimate family assets; more often than not, they are the plunder of raw political power.

• Ordinary investors are attracted by the conservative, sound financial policies practiced by Swiss bankers; they trust them more than the bankers of their native countries.

• Legitimate businesspeople and investors use Swiss banks to shield their assets from confiscatory taxation at home.

• Drug dealers, gamblers, and other not-so-legitimate types undoubtedly use Swiss banks to hide and shelter their gains.

The point is that all sorts of people use Swiss banks for all sorts of purposes; these people and these purposes range from the most noble to the most villainous. I am certain that the vast majority of the foreigners who use Swiss banks are honest, productive citizens who are merely trying to keep governments from plundering their assets. The irony of the situation is that Switzerland is so safe precisely because the plundering politicians also need it and use it, and therefore respect its sovereignty, neutrality, and confidentiality. If Switzerland didn't exist, the world would have to invent a Switzerland.

Do You Have to Report a Swiss Bank Account?

Big Brother may be banished from Switzerland, but he's alive and vigorously active in the United States. There are at least four forms and reporting requirements that pertain to someone who plans to establish a Swiss bank account.

Form 1040, Schedule B

If you itemize your deductions, you have to answer the "yes" or "no" question about whether you have a foreign bank account. Over 60 percent of U.S. taxpayers fail to do this, and I doubt that most of them are hiding secret Swiss accounts. They probably just overlook it or think it doesn't pertain to them. Failure to answer this question, however, does carry a $1,000 fine and/or a one-year prison sentence. Technically, such "noncompliance" also opens *all* of your previous income tax returns for potential audit, not just the three years covered by the Statute of Limitations. (Obviously this is one of those laws that are selectively enforced by the authorities when they're after someone.)

Form 90-22.1

If you answered "yes," you have a foreign bank account, you next have to worry about this form. The top half asks questions to establish your personal identification. You must fill this out if your foreign bank account "exceeded $1,000 in aggregate value at any time during the calendar year."

The bottom half of this form asks for details about your foreign bank, account number, amount in the account and more. You must fill this out, too, if you have more than $10,000 deposited in all your foreign accounts at any time during the calendar year. You are exempt from this reporting requirement, however, if you have a financial interest in twenty-five or more foreign accounts.

Form 4789, Currency Transaction Report

Must be filed with the IRS by your bank whenever you deposit or withdraw $10,000 or more. This applies both to foreign and domestic movements of your funds.

Form 4790, Report of International Transportation of Currency or Monetary Instruments

A customs declaration form that must be filled out any time you carry $5,000 or more in monetary instruments across the U.S. border, whether you are going out or coming in.

As I mentioned before, most banks also microfilm all your checks, because they're legally required to do this with all checks of $100 or more.

There are other reporting requirements for specific types of transactions, but these are the forms most likely to concern the individual taxpayer.

I think it is apparent that you do have to answer the question on your Form 1040 if you want to comply fully with the law. Beyond that, it depends on how you structure your Swiss-based investments. There are legal ways to avoid the other forms, and the most comprehensive, up-to-date discussion of these investment strategies will be found in Robert D. Kephart's *The Swiss System* (available for $25 from McCaffrey Enterprises, 15 Oakland Avenue, Harrison, NY 10528). Let's look briefly at a couple of these.

How to Invest Anonymously in Switzerland—Legally

The question on Form 1040, Schedule B, does not require you to disclose the location of your foreign bank account. If you are really intent on maintaining your privacy, you will not use domestic bank checks in opening or adding to your Swiss account. Instead you will use money orders, cashier's checks, or Western Union wires, paying for them in cash. You will also keep all transactions below the reportable amounts. (Full details on "How to Transfer Money Overseas" and "Getting Your Money Back" will be found in the Kephart report.)

Beyond this, you'll want to keep your Swiss bank account below $1,000 at all times, and have the bank place your other assets in types of accounts that are not reportable to the U.S. government. For example:

• *Safe-deposit accounts:* There are obvious geographical disadvantages to having a safe-deposit box this far away from home. But if you really don't think your U.S. box is that safe from confiscation, or you want to avoid having to identify your Social Security number, you can use a foreign safe-deposit box for your stocks, bonds, stamps, coins, gold, cash, diamonds, or whatever. This is not a bank account and not reportable.

• *Gold accumulation accounts:* Gold is not a taxable security as long as you hold it, and it is not a reportable bank account. You have a variety of plans from which to choose, among them Goldplan, Deak-Perera's Gold Certificate Program, and Merrill Lynch's Gold Bullion Program. You can utilize the dollar cost averaging method I recommended in Chapter 3.

• *Foreign insurance:* This is one of the most interesting ways to avoid reporting requirements, and Swiss secrecy extends to insurance accounts as well as banking accounts. At home, your records indicate only payment of an insurance premium.

For example, you can deposit your money in a Swiss-franc annuity and immediately borrow up to 90 percent of the annuity's cash value. You pay interest on the amount borrowed, but the insurance company still credits your accumulation program with interest as if 100 percent of your funds were on deposit. As a result, your net interest on the loan is likely to be just 1 to 2 percent.

With the money borrowed from your insurance annuity, you can invest anonymously (through your Swiss bank) and accumulate your assets without worrying about capital gains taxes. Switzerland has no capital gains tax, and foreign investors (such as your Swiss bank) are not taxed by the United States.

In effect, you have created a Swiss super-IRA in which you can accumulate assets on a tax-deferred basis. We will see in Chapter 13 how this lets your money grow at a much faster pace. Moreover, in addition to the secrecy, you don't need a medical examination for most types of Swiss insurance, liens cannot be attached to these assets, and there are no maximums on the coverage.

Which Swiss Bank Is for You?

You will want to do your own comparison shopping, and Harry Browne gives liquidity figures for a large number of Swiss banks in the Kephart report I've mentioned.

You may want to deal with one of the big three Swiss banks—Credit Suisse, Union Bank of Switzerland, or Swiss Bank Corporation. My own favorite is Credit Suisse, headquartered in Zurich. Credit Suisse has a significant New York operation (100 Wall Street, New York, NY 10005, telephone (212) 612-8000) where individuals and businesses may open portfolio management accounts and/or gold accounts.

In recent years, two fairly sizable Zurich banking groups have changed from private to public banks. Bank Von Tobel and Bank Julius Bar are well recognized and have an ongoing interest in developing working relationships with individuals of substance.

If you want a private bank in Zurich, my choice would be Rahn and Bodmer. In Geneva my choice might be Pictet or perhaps Lombard Odier. Hentsch, Mirabeau, Darier, and Bordier might also be considered. And in Basel, you may choose to deal with La Roche or Saragin.

Switzerland is a banking nation, with one bank office for every 1,300 inhabitants, so you have a rich variety from which to choose. One of the most delightful ways to do this, of course, is to travel to Switzerland and combine your bank shopping with a personal or family holiday. Switzerland is a scenic and cultural delight as well as your financial haven of choice in a turbulent world.

· TWELVE ·

The Well-Informed Financial Armadillo

It is said that we live in the "information age," and nowhere is this more apparent than in the field of investments. A person could spend all day engrossed in the services available—books, newspapers, magazines and newsletters, computer software, television and radio shows—and barely make a dent in the supply.

Throughout this book, I have suggested sources for the statistics and trend data you need in order to be a well-informed Financial Armadillo. You don't need to spend all day, every day, to get that information. An hour or two a week at the library is more than enough. Another way to get that information, frankly, would be to subscribe to one of my publications. In them I regularly cover and interpret the data you need to make intelligent investment decisions—data on the business cycle, inflation, the leading and coincident indicators, my Market Tension Index, and much more.

In this chapter, I will briefly suggest some of the publications you may want to investigate as you become more involved in your investments. You might consider subscribing to three or four of these, or consulting the more popular ones regularly at your library. I'll start with a rundown on my own publications since they obviously reflect the Financial Armadillo outlook expressed in this book.

Richard C. Young's Publications and Services

If you would like to keep up with my analysis and strategies on an ongoing basis, here is a complete menu of choices.

Young's World Money Forecast is my flagship economic and monetary report service for professional investors and sophisticated private investors. Each issue of the twice-monthly *YWMF* is written, printed, and mailed within twenty-four hours. In-depth analysis and strategies are offered on the stock market, the economy, U.S. Treasury securities, interest rates, currencies, inflation/deflation, and gold. Six times per year I offer a single thinly traded, closely held common-stock selection for maximum long-term profit. The *Money Forecast* has a subscription base limit of 3,500 subscribers. An initial one-year trial subscription is available for $275.

Young's International Gold Reports is my complete monthly gold service including updates on my advice on the four U.S. rare gold (one silver) collections I recommend. A one-year (12-issue) trial subscription is $75.

Richard C. Young's Intelligence Report is edited for the individual investor. The retired and soon-to-be retired investor's needs are given special attention. Model mutual fund and foundation stock portfolios are provided. Real estate for investment, retirement, and vacation needs is a regular part of *IR*. My "Big Game Hunt" stocks get steady coverage. *IR* is the service for the average investor. A year's subscription (12 issues) is $65.

My daily telephone strategy service (not a recorded message) is limited to no more than 750 total worldwide subscribers. Complete mini-updates are available on all my key indicators. A year's access to the phone service is $475.

To subscribe to any of my four financial services, send subscription advice and payment to Young Research & Publishing, Inc., Federal Building, Thames Street, Newport, RI 02840. Call in charge orders at (401) 847-4304 or (401) 849-2131.

A "Menu" of Other Financial Publications

The Wall Street Journal, P.O. Box 300, Princeton, NJ 08540. One year $114, six months $59, three months $29.50. The newspaper that covers the business, economic, and financial waterfronts. Published daily except Saturdays, Sundays, and general legal holidays.

Barron's National Business & Financial Weekly, 22 Cortlandt Street, New York, NY 10007, telephone (212) 285-5243. Dow-Jones's other, more interpretive, newspaper. Weekly, $71 per year, $1.50 per issue.

Bank Credit Analyst, 3463 Peel Street, Montreal, PQ H3A 1W7 Canada, telephone (514) 842-8518. Monthly, $475 per year, $40 per copy. Tony Boeckh provides thought-provoking commentary on the world economic and monetary system. *BCA* is not for the novice and, at $475 per year, one must have an overriding interest in the nuts and bolts of the world financial system. If you qualify on both counts, *BCA* delivers the goods.

The Wall Street Transcript, 99 Wall Street, New York, NY 10005, telephone (212) 747-9500. Weekly, $540 per year, $20 per copy. No price bargain, but then one cannot expect to receive weekly input of the quality and quantity provided by *TWST* without paying the price. Outstanding round-table discussions and brokerage reports from the best firms on Wall Street make *TWST* a one-of-a-kind publication.

William O'Neil & Company's Daily Graphs, P.O. Box 24933, Los Angeles, CA 90024, telephone (213) 820-2583. Weekly, $325 per year, $10 per copy. This is *the* chart service to have. No one does this work with the detail and number-crunching ability of Bill O'Neil's group.

Institutional Investor, Capital Cities Communications, Inc. Newspapers, 400 West 7th Street, Fort Worth, TX 76102. Editorial offices at 488 Madison Avenue, New York, NY 10022, telephone (212) 832-8888. Monthly, $95 per year, $12 per copy. Your best source of stock market ideas from the institutional point of view.

Forbes, 60 Fifth Avenue, New York, NY 10011, telephone (212) 620-2200. Published every two weeks, $39 per year, $3 per copy. Must reading for every businessperson and investor, and I'm particularly fond of David Dreman's excellent columns.

Business Week, McGraw-Hill Publications Co., Inc., 1221 Avenue of the Americas, New York, NY 10020, telephone (212) 997-1221. Weekly, $34.95 per year, $2 per copy. It has no domestic competitor. It simply does the week-to-week job of financial reporting better than any publication in America.

The Value Line Investment Survey, Value Line, Inc., 711 Third Avenue, New York, NY 10017, telephone (212) 687-3965.

Weekly, $425 per year. Provides around 135 full-page reports in each issue on leading stocks, with updated listings and summaries of 1,700 stocks in sixty-seven industries.

Standard & Poor's Stock Guide, 25 Broadway, New York, NY 10004, telephone (212) 208-8000. Monthly, $78 per year. Financial summary of over 5,100 stocks.

These last two services offer a veritable blizzard of information on more companies than the average investor can follow in a lifetime.

Once you have selected from the above "Class A" group of financial services, you may want to customize your financial library with some specialized services that target a more narrowly defined market.

If technical advice is your cup of tea, for example, take a look at John Magee, Inc.'s *Technical Stock Advisory Service,* 103 State Street, Boston, MA 02109, telephone (617) 367-0250. Weekly, $960 per year.

For a potpourri of gold information, the best bet in the field is the *Gold Newsletter,* 4425 West Napoleon Avenue, Metairie, LA 70001, telephone (504) 456-9034. Monthly, $65 per year.

If financial services with personality allow you to digest your financial news with greater comfort, I'd suggest the following. Each service has been published for well over a decade and has its own special merits.

The Professional Investor, Lynatrace, Inc., 2593 S.E. 9th Street, Pompano Beach, FL 33062, telephone (305) 946-6353. Semimonthly, $150 per year, $10 per issue. The inimitable Robert T. Gross has forgotten more about financial services than most folks will ever know. Bob is a technician and humorist at heart. He also keeps track of what some of the other services are saying. *PI* keeps close tabs on Art Merrill's excellent service as well as the latest news from other interesting services such as *Juncture Recognition.*

International Harry Schultz Letter, FERC, P.O. Box 621, CH-1001 Lausanne, Switzerland. Monthly, $260 per year. Bristles with opinion and humor, and is written in a style that would make any college English professor turn blue—a fact that is of no concern to Harry Schultz, the ultimate iconoclast.

There's simply no telling what Harry will touch upon from one issue to the next. The press often calls him a guru and the

Guinness Book of World Records touts him as the world's highest-paid investment consultant. Who knows? In any case, individualists may want to sample the *HSL*. It certainly is different!

Finally, Richard Russell's *Dow Theory Letters,* P.O. Box 1759, La Jolla, CA 92038, telephone (619) 454-0481. Semi-weekly, $225 per year. Russell has been around a long time and has developed both supporters and detractors. I've always been a supporter and, over the years, have learned valued concepts from Russell.

And One of the Biggest
Investment Bargains Around . . .

I'm referring to the American Association of Individual Investors, 612 North Michigan Avenue, Chicago, IL 60611, telephone (312) 280-0170. AAII describes itself as a "professional association for non-professionals," and explains: "We don't manage your money. We help you manage it better."

AAII's $48 annual membership fee has to be one of the greatest bargains around. Look at what you get:

• *AAII Journal,* published ten times a year. Subscription $45 per year, but free to members. A typical issue might include such topics as how holding periods affect stock risk, evaluating current tax shelters, evaluating investment newsletters, modern portfolio theory, the effect of a flat tax on investment decisions.

A special section of the *Journal* provides the results of screens that many investors use to select stocks, such as P/E ratio, debt/equity ratio, book value, and earnings growth. This can save investors considerable time in their own search.

• *The Individual Investor's Guide to No-Load Mutual Funds.* One of the best books on the subject, $19.95 but free to members. It gives in-depth analysis of over 290 funds and discusses the process of selecting funds in and out of a retirement plan.

• *AAII Personal Tax and Financial Planning Guide.* Published annually at the end of November, and free to members. It incorporates the latest laws and rulings.

• *Computerized Investing,* a bimonthly newsletter of twenty to twenty-four pages. Subscription $48 per year, but $24 to members who use computers in their investment decision making. It evaluates investment software and hardware, and features a member software exchange program.

• Seminars galore, at reduced cost to members. AAII sponsors over seventy investment seminars in cities across the United States each year. There is an introductory one-day seminar on the "Fundamentals of Investing," and advanced seminars in security analysis, real estate, financial planning, tax shelters, and mutual funds.

• Chapter meetings and special interest groups. The New York chapter, for example, has a computer users group, stock market group, real estate group, and alternative investment group, each with its own meetings and activities.

There's more, too—discounts on investment publications and investment software, special reports, and other information and materials to help you improve your investment skills. You can see why AAII has been doubling its membership each year, and now has over 100,000 members across the country!

Part V

THE FINANCIAL ARMADILLO'S LIFETIME ROAD MAP FOR FINANCIAL SUCCESS

· THIRTEEN ·

The Financial Armadillo
Plans for the Future

You may be under the impression that the U.S. Social Security system is a dead duck and you'll never see any benefits. I'm happy to tell you this is not the case, at least not given the current status of the Social Security system.

If your present annual earnings are $31,000 and you are between the ages of 56 and 60, you will—at age 65—be entitled to a monthly Social Security payment of $753. If you are at the maximum (for payment purposes) salary level of $40,000, your monthly payment will be $789.

Because of reforms made in 1983, the Social Security system is on solid ground. In fact, the Social Security trust fund earned a surplus in 1984 and 1985; when the data are in, another is likely to be reported for 1986.

More good news! Each working husband and wife is entitled to his or her own Social Security benefits. A couple (each earning the maximum $40,000) in their mid-forties will be entitled to total annual retirement benefits of approximately $22,520 at age 65.

Calculations are given in today's dollars; future inflation will increase payments. It is important to note that the current retirement age of 65 applies to workers 46 years and older. Under 46 years of age, the current retirement age is 67 years.

How much income do you need for retirement? I like to think along the lines of 60 to 80 percent of current income. This range applies to the majority of Americans. It does not apply to those in upper tax brackets, whose annual incomes are in the six-figure range.

If you have a family income of $40,000 and retire without debts (such as mortgage payments or education expenses), you should base your retirement planning on a 70-percent benchmark; thus you'd be looking for a retirement income of approximately $28,000. If you are presently in your mid-50s, Social Security will give you approximately $10,000, or 35 percent of your total funds required.

You will then need approximately $18,000 in additional annual income. Given the current six-year Treasury note yield of approximately 7 percent, you will need accumulated savings of approximately $257,000. This savings figure can be reduced substantially by any payments you will receive from a pension plan.

The Census Bureau's 1984 "Survey of Income and Program Participation" found that around 30.2 million Americans received Social Security payments at that time. Of these, 20 million—two thirds—had no other source of pension income. Clearly, you don't want to end up in this situation.

Fortunately, you won't have to if you just apply some discipline and planning. In this chapter, I will show you some of the tools you can use—IRAs, SEPs, Keoghs, and 401(k) plans. Make them a cornerstone of your Financial Armadillo Strategy and you'll be able to retire in comfort and security.

The 1986 Tax Bill

As I write, the Senate and House tax-writing committees have agreed to a sweeping revision of the nation's tax laws. Congress has not yet passed the bill, however, and all the details of the tax code revisions are not known—in many instances, they haven't been written yet.

The information in this chapter was prepared before even the outlines of the new tax bill were certain. As this book goes to press, I am noting some changes that are *proposed* for IRAs and 401(k) plans by the Senate and House conferees. Bear in mind that, as I write, these are merely proposals, that most details are not yet known, and that I have no information about changes for Keogh or SEP plans. It is always best to consult an experienced tax accountant before making pension decisions that will affect your retirement income. Considering the enormous changes being proposed in the 1986 tax bill, it is imperative that you seek such expert advice.

Individual Retirement Accounts (IRAs)

Individual retirement accounts (IRAs) have come a long way since 1982, the first year in which they became available to virtually all workers. If you are self-employed or own a business, however small, you will also want to consider the greater advantages of Keoghs, SEPs, and 401(k)s—retirement plans I will discuss after IRAs. But for most Americans, IRAs are a very good solution to the inadequacy of Social Security.

IRAs are retirement funds that come in all manner of shapes and sizes. You can open them at mutual fund companies, brokerage houses, banks, savings and loan institutions, federally chartered credit unions, and insurance companies. With IRAs you can invest in stocks, bonds, annuities, bank certificates or accounts, Treasury and other government securities, mutual funds (stock, bond, and money market funds), or any combination of these investments.

In line with the philosophy I've emphasized in this book, I recommend that you open *self-directed* IRAs. These are accounts that allow *you* to decide which investments to make, when to make them, and when to shift them to reflect changes in economic conditions and the business cycle. The mutual fund "families" suggested in Chapter 6 are good places to open such self-directed accounts, since they allow you to switch between different types of stock, bond, and money market funds with the greatest of ease. The Benham funds recommended in Chapter 2 are another good choice.

Another excellent choice for your IRAs is Charles Schwab & Co., the nation's first and largest discount brokerage firm. Schwab gives IRA holders one of the largest arrays of investment vehicles—over 160 no-load and low-load mutual funds, as well as the entire panoply of individual stocks and bonds available to all investors. In addition, there is never a minimum amount you are required to contribute; there are no set-up, maintenance, or termination fees; you can move from one investment to another with no penalty fees; you can save up to 75 percent on brokerage commissions; you get twenty-four-hour service and comprehensive monthly statements; and your IRA assets at Schwab are protected up to $2,500,000 through the SIPC* and Aetna Casualty & Surety Company (limited to

*Securities Investor Protection Corporation, established by the U.S. Congress.

$100,000 for claims in cash). *For more information:* Charles Schwab & Co., Inc., One Second Street, San Francisco, CA 94105, telephones (800) 227-4444 (out of state), (800) 792-0988 (in state), and (415) 546-1000 (local).

The Advantages of an IRA

Under current (1986) law, you get two major benefits from an IRA. First, your contributions are tax deductible in the year made. Second, your assets are tax deferred until you withdraw them, allowing more rapid growth through income compounding and appreciation. Both are considerable benefits.

If you are in the 35 percent tax bracket ($25,000 income for a single person or $40,000 for a married couple filing jointly) you will save $700 in taxes by contributing $2,000 to an IRA. In essence, it costs you only $1,300 to establish a $2,000 IRA, since the rest would have gone to taxes anyway. The main advantage, though, is the accelerated capital accumulation that is possible with the tax deferral. A couple contributing $4,000 a year, and compounding it at 10 percent, will have $229,000 after 20 years. If they were in the 40 percent tax bracket and doing this outside the IRA, their total after-tax contribution would have amounted to only about $48,000.

If the 1986 tax bill is passed as proposed, everyone still will be able to accumulate their IRA contributions on a tax-deferred basis. That's very important to remember. Whether your annual contribution will also be tax-deductible in the year made, however, will depend on your employment status and income level. If you are *not* covered by some employer pension plan, you keep the full deduction whatever your income. If you *are* covered by an employer pension plan, you keep the full deduction only if your adjusted gross income is below $40,000 on a joint return, or below $25,000 for a single individual; you get a partial deduction if your adjusted gross income is between $40,000 and $50,000 on a joint return, or between $25,000 and $35,000 for a single individual; and you get no deduction if your income is above those levels.

I repeat, the *main* advantage of an IRA is that your accumulation grows faster because it is tax-deferred, and that advantage remains intact under the proposed tax bill. Never underestimate the power of compounding. The key is to start early and continue saving on a regular basis. An individual contributing $2,000 a year to an IRA that compounds at 10 percent will have $114,540 in 20 years, $328,980 in 30 years, and $885,180 in 40 years. Increase that yield to 12 percent and this individual earns $144,100 in 20 years, $482,660 in 30 years, and $1,534,180 in 40 years.

If you are young, you may scoff at what a million will be worth in 40 years. One thing is for certain, however: You'll be better off with that million than without it.

Some Basics About IRAs

How much can you contribute? An individual may contribute up to $2,000 of earned income to an IRA each year. If you earn only $2,000 a year, you can contribute all of it.

A married couple where both work may contribute up to $4,000 a year, but neither spouse can contribute more than $2,000 a year.

A married couple where only one works may contribute up to $2,250 a year. There must be two separate accounts. You can divide the $2,250 any way you wish, so long as no account is more than $2,000.

You do not have to contribute each year. If you miss a year, though, you cannot "make it up" by contributing more than the allowable amount in a subsequent year.

Your contributions must be based on income received for personal services—salary, wages, commissions, tips, fees, bonuses, or self-employed earned income. Alimony may also be counted. You cannot use income from investments (interest, dividends, capital gains, rents) in determining how much you may contribute.

How long can you contribute? When must you start withdrawing? You may contribute to your IRA each year in which you have sufficient earned income, up to the year you reach age 70½, at which time you *must* start withdrawing from your IRA. This is because Congress intended this to be a retirement plan, not an estate plan. You *may* start withdrawing without penalty from your IRA at age 59½ if you wish.

What happens if you withdraw funds earlier? If you withdraw funds before age 59½, you must pay a penalty of 10 percent of the amount withdrawn. You also pay regular income tax on the amount withdrawn that year. There is no penalty if you become permanently disabled.

How many IRAs may you have? You may have as many as you wish, but you may not contribute a total of more than $2,000 each year.

When can you contribute to your IRA each year? You may do so anytime during that calendar year and until you file your income tax on April 15 of the following year. You must contribute to your IRA by April 15 even if you file for an extension in paying the income tax.

You do not have to make your entire contribution at once. You can have a payroll deduction plan, or use dollar cost averaging on a regular basis if you wish. Just be certain you don't exceed $2,000 per year in total contributions.

Eight IRA Tips and Strategies

1. *It pays to invest early.* The sooner you make your contribution, the sooner it begins to appreciate tax-free. Assume a $2,000 IRA contribution annually for 30 years, earning 10 percent. If you made each contribution on January 1, your account will be worth $361,886 at the end of those 30 years. If you wait until December 31 each year to make your contribution, that figure goes down to $328,988. And if you wait each year until the following April 15, you earn only $319,548—$42,338 less than if you were a January 1st early bird.

2. *Make the most of your spouse's IRA.* Remember that compounding increases your returns with each year. If you place most of your $2,250 contribution in the younger spouse's account, therefore, it will accrue tax-free earnings for a longer period of time—until that spouse reaches age 70½. Just make certain neither partner's IRA receives more than $2,000 a year.

Similarly, a working person older than 70½ cannot make contributions for himself or herself, but may continue making contributions up to $2,000 a year for a nonworking spouse who is under age 70½.

3. *Minimize the amounts you must withdraw.* When you become 70½, your annual withdrawals are supposed to be large enough to deplete your account over your life expectancy or the joint life expectancy of you and your spouse. This is because Congress intended IRAs to be for retirement, not for establishing an estate. If you don't need all the money for current living expenses, however, there are ways to minimize the amount you must withdraw each year, and perhaps leave more to your beneficiary.

First, you can refigure your and your spouse's life expectancy each year. That reduces the annual minimum since, each year, your theoretical date of death is pushed further into the future.

Secondly, you can pick someone younger as your beneficiary— a child, or grandchild, or even someone not related—and use your joint life expectancy to stretch payments even further. If you do this with someone who is not your spouse, though, you cannot refigure your beneficiary's life expectancy each year. Also, more than half of your current account must be projected to be paid to you over your life expectancy. You will probably need an accountant's help in figuring this out to stay within the law.

4. *Don't gamble with your IRA funds.* Conservative to aggressive strategies are permissible, depending on your age and financial situation, but you shouldn't gamble with your IRA money. These are retirement funds, not play money or speculation funds, and a loss within your IRA portfolio is not tax deductible.

5. *Don't overtrade with your IRA funds.* The same rules apply here as outside your IRA portfolio. Invest for the long term; don't be a trader. Most people are not successful traders, and even if you are mildly successful, the commissions can eat up those profits. Again, remember that IRA dollars are more valuable than non-IRA dollars since they accumulate and compound tax free. Don't waste them away with trading commissions.

6. *Don't waste tax shelters in your IRA.* If you buy tax-free municipal bonds, for example, they should be bought outside your IRA in order to maintain the tax-free advantage. Everything taken out of an IRA is taxable *when* it's taken out, even earnings from tax-free securities.

7. *You can get around "prohibited" investments.* You may not invest IRA funds directly in collectibles, including gold and

silver.* You can, however, invest in precious metals funds or mining stocks. Similarly, you may not invest IRA funds directly in real estate, but you can buy into real estate limited partnerships. Also, you cannot buy insurance with your IRA, but you can buy a fixed-rate annuity from an insurance company.

8. *You can pay for your IRA with your IRS refund.* If you cannot contribute earlier, you theoretically can file early with the IRS claiming an IRA deduction, receive a tax refund, and use that refund to pay for your IRA contribution before April 15.

What Kinds of Investments Belong in Your IRA?

When IRAs first became available, most people put their money in a bank or thrift institution's certificate of deposit (CD). Since then three trends have altered the picture.

First, those who began establishing IRAs in 1982 and have done so each year now have $10,000, more or less, in their IRAs. With that much money involved, they look at their investments differently and are ready to diversify.

Secondly, many types of investment vehicles (such as mutual funds) have gone after these IRA accounts. Sometimes they've altered their characteristics to become attractive for IRAs.

Third, interest rates have declined, making CD returns seem puny compared with other investment returns. As a result, there's been a noticeable shift toward more aggressive types of investments.

With this increasing competition for hundreds of billions in IRA dollars, you will get all sorts of arguments about what belongs in an IRA. Before the 1986 tax bill, income was taxed at a top rate of 50 percent while long-term capital gains were taxed at a top rate of 20 percent. Thus the consensus was that IRAs were the place to shelter income-producing debt instruments such as money market funds, taxable bonds, bank CDs, mortgage-backed securities, and the like; and that equity instruments, such as stocks and real estate, belonged outside IRAs

---

*Under the proposed 1986 tax bill, gold or silver coins issued by the United States government would be eligible IRA investments, but other collectibles would remain ineligible.

because of the lower long-term capital gains tax rate. Under the proposed 1986 tax bill, however, capital gains income will be taxed at the same rate as other income (the top rate on both will be 28 percent). Thus IRAs may become a practical way for upper-income people who lose deductions to shelter capital gains appreciation.

Three Ways to Transfer IRAs

As your IRA assets grow and diversify, you will want to shift them around to reflect changing economic and business conditions, or perhaps split the funds in one type of investment vehicle among several different investment vehicles. There are three ways to make such transfers of your IRA assets, and you must be aware of the regulations in order to avoid penalties.

Bear in mind the distinction between your IRAs and their *trustees* or *custodians*. Each individual IRA was initiated with just $2,000 or less, but hopefully is growing much larger. The trustee or guardian is the financial institution handling that IRA—a mutual fund company, brokerage house, bank, insurance company, savings and loan institution, or credit union. You may have many different IRAs that are handled by the same trustee, or each IRA may be handled by a different trustee.

Now, for the three types of transfers.

First, there's the in-house switch. Within the same institution, you change from a money market fund to a stock fund, for example, or from stocks to bonds. The regulations allow you to make as many of these switches as you want, whenever you want. This is a major advantage of having your IRA with a mutual fund "family" or a discount brokerage house.

The second kind of switch is from one trustee to another, where you never see the money. For example, you sign the forms and ask your bank to transfer your IRA to a mutual fund company. Again, the regulations allow you to make as many of these switches as you want. A major problem, though, is the amount of time these transfers sometimes take—perhaps months. Fees may also be charged.

The third kind of IRA switch is from one trustee to you, then from you to a different trustee. When you take possession of the money, it is called a *rollover*. This is often quicker than a trustee-to-trustee transfer, but you are allowed to do this only once every 12 months without a penalty. (We're talking about 12 months between rollovers, not the 12-month calendar year.) A second rollover within 12 months is treated as an early withdrawal if you are under age 59½, so you would owe income tax plus a 10 percent penalty on the amount involved in the second rollover. Also, when you take possession of money in any rollover, you must reinvest it within 60 days in another IRA or face these penalties.

Keogh Plans

Keogh plans are basically super-IRAs for self-employed persons. The ground rules are pretty much the same as for IRAs, except that you can contribute much more each year.

As with IRAs, your annual contributions are tax deductible, and they remain tax deferred until you withdraw the funds in retirement. The minimum age for withdrawal without penalty is 59½, and you must start withdrawing once you reach age 70½. You cannot borrow from your Keogh funds. With a Keogh, however, you can contribute as much as 20 percent of your net self-employment income or $30,000, whichever is less. Let's look at what this means for your retirement.

The Power of Tax-Deferred Accumulation

Let's assume that you are in a 40 percent tax bracket* and that you invest $10,000 each year, earning a return of 10 percent each year.

If you do not have a tax-deferred plan (such as a Keogh), you must pay taxes from the account each year. At the end of 25 years, you will have accumulated $286,362. It's better to have that sum than not to have it, but it's not much to show for contributions totaling $250,000.

Now let's say you put this $10,000 into a tax-deferred Keogh plan, earning the same 10 percent return. At the end of 25 years you will have accumulated $983,470.

---

*This is before the proposed 1986 tax bill would lower the maximum tax rate to 28 percent.

That's the power of tax-deferred accumulation: $983,470 versus $286,362—an increase of $697,108!

Who Can Have a Keogh Plan?

Here are some types of people who should consider establishing Keogh plans:
• Sole proprietors who file a Schedule C with their tax returns.
• Partners who file a Schedule K.
• Self-employed individuals who earn income from services rendered or products produced and sold, either full time or part time.
• Freelancers who provide outside services for income.
• Subchapter S corporations.
• Members of corporate boards of directors.

Partners, it should be noted, cannot establish separate plans; it is the partnership, as "employer," that must establish the plan for all of the partners. And if you have employees, you'll have to provide similar Keogh funds for your employees.

Three Kinds of Defined-Contribution Plans

Defined-contribution plans are the simplest kind of Keogh plans to set up. You have three basic choices:

Money purchase
You determine a fixed percentage-of-earnings formula for your annual contribution. The problem here is that you must contribute the same percentage each year unless your business shows a loss. If you don't do this, or fall short, there are heavy penalties from the IRS.

Profit sharing
You decide each year whether you will contribute to your plan, and how much. This gives you the flexibility you need, but the limit you may contribute annually is 15 percent of earned income (not 20 percent) or $30,000, whichever is less.

Paired plan
You can combine the two plans to maximize your contributions while retaining some flexibility. Figure out the base-level percent-

age you think you can contribute comfortably even in slim-earnings years. Open your money purchase plan with that percentage, then contribute additionally to your profit sharing plan as your budget allows. The combined maximum for the two plans remains 20 percent of earned income or $30,000, whichever is less.

A Plan for the Older Investor Who Must Accumulate Quickly

What if you are approaching 50 years of age or more, and haven't provided for your retirement? You are making an excellent income, however, and could sock away most of it if there were a way to do this tax-deferred.

Fortunately for you, there *is* a way to do this. It's called a defined-*benefit* plan. With a defined-benefit plan, you figure out what you will need to achieve an annual retirement income equal to the average of your highest earnings over three consecutive years. To reach that target, you can contribute as much as 100 percent of your earnings to your Keogh, up to $90,000 per year.

This type of plan requires the services of an accountant to determine your annual contributions, but it's worth it to get your retirement fund accumulated quickly.

Some Notes About Keoghs

IRAs: You can have a Keogh in addition to your IRA.

Deadlines: When you first set up your Keogh, you must get it established by December 31. You then have until the due date of your tax return to make your contribution. If you get an extension for filing your tax return, the later date is also your deadline for making Keogh contributions.

Hard assets: With a defined-benefit Keogh plan, you can legally purchase hard assets such as gold, silver, and numismatic coins.

Lump-sum withdrawals: If you have had your Keogh plan for at least five years, and are age 59½ or older, you can withdraw sums in a lump sum and be eligible for 10-year forward averaging.

With 10-year forward averaging, you pay all the tax within one year of the distribution, but it is taxed as though you were receiving the payout over 10 years. This reduces considerably the amount of tax you must pay. Here's an example of how it works: If you withdraw a lump sum of $100,000, you divide that sum by 10. The money is taxed at the rate in the tax tables for $10,000, without regard to total income, deductions, or exemptions. Then the tax owed is simply multiplied by ten.

401(k) Plans

The name comes from Section 401(k) of the Internal Revenue Code, which permits businesses, both incorporated and nonincorporated, to set up these plans. You'll soon realize why these are one of the most popular and fastest-growing corporate retirement plans in the United States.

Under present (1986) law, employees may set aside as much as 20 percent of their salary, with a maximum of $30,000 a year. With most corporate plans, employee contributions are made in after-tax dollars. With a 401(k), the amount contributed is deducted from your salary *before* applying taxes. For the employee, this means lower taxes. For the employer, it may reduce the amount that must be paid for Social Security, workers' compensation, and unemployment insurance.

There are other advantages of the 401(k) under present law:

• You can borrow against your 401(k) funds without penalty, provided you demonstrate a "hardship" financial need. Such "hardships," however, can include buying a home, paying for your children's education, or unusual medical expenses. You may borrow up to 50 percent of your vested account balance, with a ceiling of $50,000.

• Such loans must be paid back with interest within five years, or when you leave the company (if that's earlier). However, the employer can set a low interest rate (Citibank charges its employees 5 percent interest). Also, this interest is deductible on your current income tax return, even though it is credited back to your 401(k) account. *You are paying yourself interest, and that interest is tax-deductible!*

• Lump-sum withdrawals at retirement are taxed on a ten-year tax averaging basis, exclusive of any other income you may be receiving at that time. This usually reduces your taxes enormously over the five-year averaging allowed for IRAs.

Under the proposed 1986 tax bill, the maximum annual 401(k) contribution would drop to $7,000; early withdrawals would be subject to a 10 percent penalty, just as with early withdrawals from IRAs; and the interpretation of a "hardship" withdrawal would be much stricter, limited to medical emergencies and the like.

Plans may be designed to allow for employee contributions only, for employer contributions, or for a combination where the employer matches the employees' contributions.

A possible disadvantage of 401(k) plans is their anti-discrimination provision—meaning that all employees, not just the top officers, must be covered on basically the same terms. You may not be prepared financially for that sort of obligation. This is no problem, of course, if your corporation consists of you or you and your spouse. Another possible solution is to lease other workers (besides you and your spouse) from one of the employee-leasing firms spreading around the country. You institute a 401(k) for yourself, and the leased workers get their benefits from the employee-leasing firm.

Another disadvantage of 401(k) plans—if you're just an employee, not an owner of the corporation—is that the employer decides where and how to invest the funds contributed to the plan.

Simplified Employee Pensions (SEPs)

Still another alternative for employers, including self-employed individuals who have incorporated, is the simplified employee pension (SEP). This is basically a super-IRA, and in fact is also referred to as a SEP-IRA.

Advantages of the SEP-IRA

• Much less paperwork than with a Keogh or 401(k) plan. It lives up to its name.
• It puts the ball back in the employee's court: The employee sets up an IRA wherever he or she wants, and the employer contributes to that IRA. That means you can specify a *self-directed* IRA.
• Contribution limits are much higher than with a regular IRA. The employer may contribute up to 15 percent of an employee's salary, with a maximum of $30,000. The employee can

add $2,000 on top of this. Just let the IRA's trustee know this is a SEP-IRA, so they'll admit the larger amounts.

• Unlike regular IRAs, the employer can continue to make tax-deductible contributions to the SEP for workers who are over age 70½.

Disadvantages of the SEP-IRA

• You cannot borrow against these funds, and you face the usual IRA penalties for early withdrawals.

• Lump-sum distributions do not qualify for 10-year income averaging, and thus are taxable as ordinary income.

Which Plan for You?

Which plan is best for you? When you go beyond the simple IRA, I suggest you talk to your tax accountant to determine the answer to that question. I've been able to give you just a broad outline of what is available. The important point is to do *something,* and start *now.*

· FOURTEEN ·

The Financial Armadillo's Lifetime Road Map for Financial Success

Your ability to set aside investment funds will vary as you proceed through life. So will your financial needs. Your investment portfolio should reflect these changing conditions. Most of us follow a general pattern of four investment stages during our adult life. In this final chapter I will show you how the Financial Armadillo Strategy adapts to these stages to give you a lifetime road map for financial success.

First review Table 18, "The Financial Armadillo's Investment Rating Chart." This will refresh your memory about the different types of investments we have covered and will help put them in perspective. Treasury bills and gold are the linchpins of the Financial Armadillo's protective coat of armor, while mutual funds and individual stocks are the armadillo's "claws" digging for profits. The proportions of these different types of investments will change with the four stages, or "seasons," of your investment life.

Bear in mind that this chapter deals with the changing life cycle. Within each stage of your life cycle, you will also want to change your portfolio mix to take account of the business cycle and inflation. If we have another period of double-digit inflation, for example, you'll want to beef up your position in gold. Similarly, the depths of recession are the best time to emphasize stocks and equity mutual funds.

A Financial Road Map for the Spring Years of Your Life

The key here is to get out of the gate fast on a thoroughbred. You want to put time and compounding on your side.

During this stage you are fresh out of college or high school, and have started working at your first job. You are probably single; if married, you probably have not started your family yet. Money seems to slip through your fingers, and the last thing on your mind is putting away some of it for investments. Think again!

I know that retirement seems a world away, and you have big plans for business success that will allow you to salt away big money later on. That's great, but the key to your financial success is to start *now*. Don't wait until you think you can "afford" to invest, and here are two good reasons why:

1. Right now you may not be able to invest more than $2,000, your IRA maximum, each year. Later in life you'll probably be able to afford much more. By starting now, however, no matter how small the amount of your funds, you are giving yourself a lesson that cannot be bought or duplicated—*experience* in managing your investments.

Learn and make your initial mistakes now, while your investment portfolio is relatively small. Your mistakes will cost you much less now than later! And when your portfolio has grown much larger, you'll be able to get better performance with less risk to that more valuable investment pie.

2. Time is money, and I'm referring here to the power of compounded interest or return. The longer your money works for you—especially in a tax-deferred IRA—the greater your returns. You're not impressed? Well, I know retirement seems an eternity away, so let's just think in terms of ten years. Ten years can pass by very fast. Let's see just what a difference ten years can make.

Let's assume you invest $2,000 each year in your IRA, and earn a 10 percent return, compounded annually. You plan to retire at age 65. Here's what you will have then, if you . . .

• start at age 25, letting your money work 40 years for you: *$885,180*

• start at age 35, letting your money work 30 years for you: *$328,980*

You will lose $556,200 in net retirement worth, just by procrastinating those 10 years!

It's twice as bad, of course, if you are married and both spouses work. Let's see what $4,000 in two IRAs each year will do:

• Start at age 25, letting your money work 40 years for the two of you: *$1,770,360*

• Start at age 35, letting your money work 30 years for the two of you: *$657,960*

You and your spouse will lose $1,112,400 in net retirement worth, just by procrastinating those 10 years!

Do you really want to throw away more than a million dollars? I hope not! Are you convinced that your IRA is more important than that flashy new car or a VCR? I hope so!

Now that I have your attention, let me also stress that this is the best time of your life to go into business for yourself. I do not believe in working for someone else. You have seen what $2,000 or $4,000 a year can do for you, if you start now. With your own corporation you'll be able to salt away much more—perhaps as much as $30,000 a year in a Keogh plan, as we saw in Chapter 13. Imagine what *that* will do for your net worth in a few years! Of course, you won't be able to start with contributions that big, but with your own corporation you won't be limited to $2,000 or $4,000 a year, and your tax-deferred investments will be able to grow with your business success.

In conclusion, this is what you must do during the spring season of your investment life:

1. Start your IRA as soon as possible. If you are married and both you and your spouse work, start both IRAs as soon as possible. Contribute to them at the very beginning of each year—don't lose any of that compounding!

2. Become self-employed and start your own corporation if possible. Set up a tax-deferred pension plan so you can increase your savings dramatically.

3. Emphasize growth stocks and funds at this stage of life. You can afford risk better now than later, and you'll have more years for all that growth to work for you. Partners Fund or the Evergreen Total Return Fund would be good examples of good initial investments.

4. Start your good financial habits now. Start on day one with your IRA. Don't trade—invest for long-term capital gains.

Stay well informed, and learn from your mistakes as well as your successes.

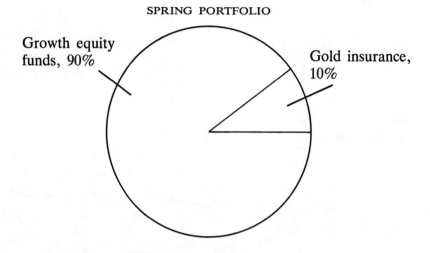

SPRING PORTFOLIO

Growth equity funds, 90%

Gold insurance, 10%

A Financial Road Map for the Summer Years of Your Life

It's time for a tune-up! You are advancing in your own business or career, and a growing family is probably putting pressures on your growing salary. The important thing is to keep the momentum going that you started earlier, and hopefully add some new investments.

As soon as you have some excess money to invest, put it in the "big game hunt" I described in Chapter 7. As always, buy for the long term; don't trade. But also buy for the big hits. We're not talking IBM or General Foods here, but high-growth areas such as biotechnology. Yes, they're also high risk, as I pointed out in Chapter 7, but now is the time to take the risk and grow with your winners.

Do your homework, select ten of your best prospects, then stay with each of them until you have a very good reason not to. Unless you are very successful in your business and have plenty of funds to invest, stick to ten stocks in your big game portfolio. If you buy another stock, sell one.

SUMMER PORTFOLIO

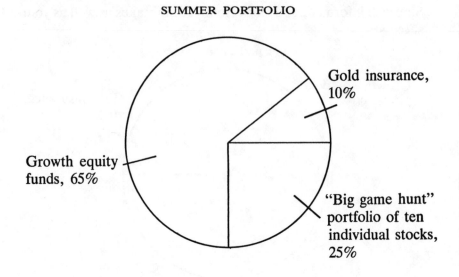

Gold insurance, 10%

Growth equity funds, 65%

"Big game hunt" portfolio of ten individual stocks, 25%

A Financial Road Map for the Autumn Years of Your Life

You are now in your peak earning years, but you are also thinking seriously about retirement for the first time. It's just fifteen, ten, or fewer years away, so you will want to become more concerned about the protection of your principal. You still want growth, of course, but you also want to dampen the volatility of your portfolio and play it safer.

Now, for the first time, you will add Treasury notes to your portfolio. The right ones will have maturities of from one to 10 years, and you'll choose them using the method I gave you in Chapter 5.

In the stock portion of your portfolio, emphasize the value approach in your new selections. If your portfolio has grown as planned, you can maintain your ten-stock "big game hunt," but add to your "foundation portfolio" (see Chapter 7) until it constitutes 50 percent or more of all your individual stock assets.

AUTUMN PORTFOLIO

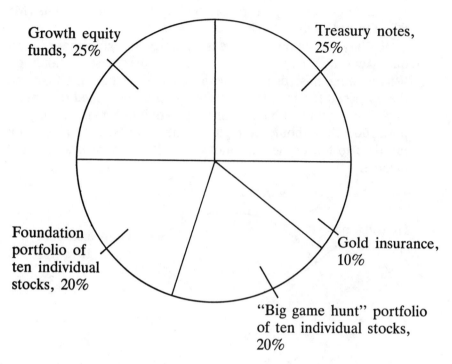

Growth equity funds, 25%

Treasury notes, 25%

Foundation portfolio of ten individual stocks, 20%

Gold insurance, 10%

"Big game hunt" portfolio of ten individual stocks, 20%

A Financial Road Map for the Winter Years of Your Life

You are now ready to retire! To give you security during those retirement years, we want to build a veritable fortress of protection.

How do we get absolute, ironclad security of principal and insurance against inflation? With Treasury notes and gold, of course. How much of your retirement portfolio will be in T-notes and gold? As much as necessary.

The first step is to determine your annual cash income needs (*not* desires). You choose the right T-notes to buy, using the method I gave you in Chapter 5, and figure out how much you must invest in T-notes to get the annual yield you need. That's how much you buy of Treasury securities.

The second indispensable element of your retirement portfolio is the gold insurance. It should constitute approximately 10 percent of your portfolio and be held as certificates, fine common date U.S. rare gold pieces such as the Saint-Gaudens (MS 60). Do not hold gold shares.

To buy the amount of Treasury notes and gold that you require, you may have to sell most or all of your stock holdings. When doing this, dispense with the riskiest equities first and then proceed toward the safer ones. If you don't need to convert everything, you will have your safest equities remaining in your portfolio. They should be high-income equities, too. This is not the time to bet on new technologies; all you want is safety and income.

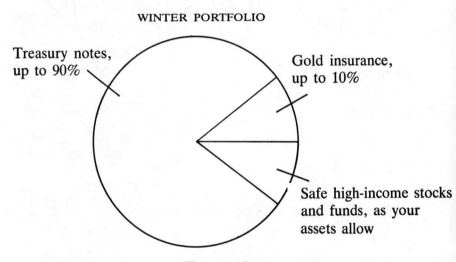

WINTER PORTFOLIO

Treasury notes, up to 90%

Gold insurance, up to 10%

Safe high-income stocks and funds, as your assets allow

TABLE 18
The Financial Armadillo's Investment Rating* Chart

TYPE OF INVESTMENT	SAFETY	POTENTIAL RETURN (INCOME/GROWTH)	COMMENTS
Treasury bills	5	1	Your "risk-free" investment. While T-bills now offer historically high *real* return after inflation, that return is still lower than with riskier investments. See Chapter 2.

*1 to 5 armadillos, 5 being "safest" or "best return."

Treasury notes (short-term)	4	2	Slightly more risk, slightly more income than T-bills. Combine bills and notes for best results.
Treasury bonds	1	1	Very likely will have no *real* return after inflation, thus not for Financial Armadillos. Avoid.
Gold	5	0–5 (rises with inflation)	The ultimate inflation hedge. Will get no armadillos for return in noninflationary times, but 5 in periods of hyperinflation. See Chapter 3 for best *ways* to invest and get those 5 armadillos for safety.
Silver	Rises with inflation	Rises with inflation	It's not gold, so *both* safety and return will rise with inflation. See Chapter 4.
Mutual funds	4	4	See Chapter 6 for ways to pick the right funds and maximize safety and return.
Individual stocks (foundation portfolio)	4	4	Safety comes with diversification. See Chapter 7 for ways to maximize safety and return.
Individual stocks (big game hunt)	2	5	See Chapter 7.
Stock options	1	5	For "play" funds (gambling funds) only. See Chapter 8.

· Index ·